# SHANGHAI

上海市旅游事业管理委员会　中国旅游出版社　编

**Compiled by Shanghai Tourism Administrations and China Travel & Tourism Press**

《中国旅游全览》（系列）编辑委员会

编委会主任：何光昕
副 主 任：孙 钢　张希钦　顾朝曦
　　　　　王 军　佟华龄　肖潜辉

《上海》分册编委会

主　　编：姚明宝
副 主 编：道书明　朱承蓉　范能船
责任编辑：吕大千
中文撰稿：范云兴　孙 蕾
英文翻译：胡志挥
装帧设计：布尉清　白志勇
地图编辑：孙素菊
摄　　影：（按姓氏笔划排序）
　　　　　王钢锋　叶天荣　白志勇　达向群　孙建忠
　　　　　纪海鹰　吕大千　李志成　杨中俭　陈东成
　　　　　陆 杰　陆明华　杨建中　陈 盛　张 颖
　　　　　邵黎阳　张 潮　夏云鹏　祖忠人　郭一江
　　　　　谢新发　薛长命　欧阳鹤

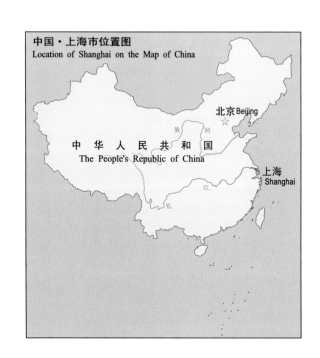

中国·上海市位置图
Location of Shanghai on the Map of China

北京 Beijing

中华人民共和国
The People's Republic of China

上海
Shanghai

**图书在版编目（CIP）数据**

上海／本社编．－北京：中国旅游出版社，
2001.10
（中国旅游全览）
ISBN 7-5032-1889-4

Ⅰ．上… Ⅱ．本… Ⅲ．旅游指南－上海－画册
Ⅳ.K928.951-64

中国版本图书馆 CIP 数据核字 （ 2001）第 064682 号

**上 海**

中国旅游出版社出版
地址：北京建国门内大街甲 9 号
邮政编码：100005 电话：65201010
北京利丰雅高长城电分制版中心制版
东莞新扬印刷有限公司印刷
2001 年 10 月第一版　第一次印刷
开本：787 × 1092 毫米 1/12 印张 10
印数：1-5000 册 中英对照 精装:0012800

# 目　　录

# CONTENTS

# 序 言

上海市旅游事业管理委员会 — 姚明宝

上海，确实是海内外人士向往的都市。滔滔黄浦江，汩汩苏州河，令人遐想不绝。

六千年前，最早的上海人便在今崧泽古文化遗址繁衍生息。战国四君子之一春申君，即封于上海地区，故上海亦称"申"。上海原是滨海村。史载东晋时虞潭在海上"修沪渎垒"。"沪"是捕鱼的工具，江河流入海者为渎。所以上海又称沪。元至元二十八年(公元1291年)上海正式建城。"衣被天下"的纺织始祖黄道婆，就在此改革纺织技术。明代，依托港口而兴旺，已享有"江海通津"、"东南都会"的盛誉。引进西方科技的先驱徐光启，也生活在这块土地上。19世纪二三十年代，申城崛起，"十里洋场"被称为"东方纽约"、"东方巴黎"。然而，近现代史叱咤风云的杰出人物，也无不在此留下足迹。

而今，上海"一年一个样，三年大变样"，正在实现跨越式的发展，不仅要成为国际经济、金融、贸易和航运中心，而且要成长为太平洋西岸有文化特色的国际旅游城市。上海成了开放之都、时尚之都、动感之都。她犹如盛开的白玉兰，朵朵向上，呈现出生机勃勃的开路先锋、奋发向上的精神。

上海市的都市风光，使人目不暇接。黄浦江两畔的外滩，以其"万国建筑博览"的美名传誉世界；其东畔，如果登上东方明珠广播电视塔、金茂大厦，则数千幢鳞次栉比的高楼大厦满目辉煌，真是沧海巨变一览无遗。作为核心地区的人民广场、上海博物馆、上海大剧院、上海城市规划展示馆等，现代的气息和华夏文化以及海派文化的底蕴融为一体。上海的现代化并没有忘却自己的历史文化，豫园等历史文化风貌保存完好。中共一大会址、毛泽东寓所、孙中山、宋庆龄、鲁迅等一大批纪念地、名人故居也整新如故。市郊不但是探古访幽的好去处，也是休闲度假的胜地。上海的夜景尤其迷人，壮观、繁华、气派、温馨、流动。充满生机，可与国外著名的大都市媲美。

建筑是"石头的历史"、"凝固的音乐"。从传统建筑到近代石库门建筑，从近代西洋建筑到当代的现代建筑，从地铁、轻轨、立交桥到内环高架、外环高架、延安路高架，都诉说着历史的嬗变，演奏着都市巨变的交响曲。大片城市绿地的不断营造，更体现出上海永续发展的决心。

漫步南京路步行街、高雅的淮海路，游憩于豫园商城、徐家汇商城、上海火车站不夜城、浦东新世纪商城，橱窗、灯光、商品，乃至于熙熙攘攘、川流不息的人群，也成了都市一道道亮丽的风景线。证券市场，人头攒动，目光闪闪，更显示了都市人独有的经济头脑和拼搏气质。

都市生活是快节奏的，同时文化娱乐也是五光十色，轻松而充满乐趣。传统的文化娱乐依然存在，但时尚的文化娱乐更是层出不穷。特别是在春节、"五一"、"十一"黄金旅游周，以及众多的旅游节庆，如"迎元旦，撞龙华晚钟"、"龙华庙会"、"南汇桃花节"、"上海国际茶文化节"、"上海桂花节"、"上海旅游节"、"上海国际电影节"等节庆活动中，上海的民俗风情更是千姿百态，展现无穷魅力和鲜明的海派特色。

"吃在上海"更是名不虚传。本帮菜、扬帮

菜、徽帮菜、杭帮菜、甬帮菜、京津菜、苏锡菜、粤菜、川菜、闽菜、豫菜、潮州菜、香港菜、澳门菜、台湾菜、素食菜、清真菜、日本料理、韩国料理、欧美菜等应有尽有。特色小吃、家常菜、本帮菜颇具上海本地特色。上海不愧为美食家的乐园。

　　漫游大都市上海，可带来无与伦比的享受，也可带来为之振奋的激励。享受的是活力，激励的也是活力。就像那滔滔黄浦江、汩汩苏州河，逝者如斯夫，不舍昼夜!

1.上海市市花——白玉兰
Yulan (magnolia), Shanghai's municipal flower.

2.人民广场
People's Square.

# Foreword

YaoMingbao(ShanghaiTourismAdministrations)

Shanghai is really a fascinating metropolis for tourists from both home and abroad. At the sight of the bustling Huangpu River and the magnificent Suzhou Creek, you will soon have a series of fantastic reveries.

Six thousand years ago, the place was the site of Songze Culture and it was precisely on this land that the forefathers of Shanghai had labored, lived and multiplied. Duuring the Warring States period (475-221 B.C.), the soverign of the State of Chu gave this land to Prince Chun Shen as a fief, Shanghai was therefore named "Shen". Soon after this land had become a fishing village during the East Jin Dynasty (317-420), Yu Tan, a local official, built a fishing facility at the mouth of a river, so the place was known as "Wu" (literary: a fishing instrument). In the 28th year of the reign of Zhiyuan (1290) during the Yuan Dynasty (1271-1368), Shanghai was formally built into a city. Before long, with the appearance of Huang Daopo, a legendary figure who invented the spinning wheel and reformed the technique of cotton weaving, Shanghai gained thereby the fame of "its production of clothes being on sale throughout the country." By the time of the Ming Dynasty (1368-1644), with the backing of its port, Shanghai began to flourish, enjoying widespread renown as the "bustling port and grand metropolis in the Southeast". Meanwhile, Xu Guangqi (1562-1633), a noted pioneer who had introduced the Western science and technique into China, was born and lived in Shanghai. Ever since its rising to prominence during the twenties and the thirties of last century, Shanghai, the "Paradise of Adventurers", was acclaimed as "the New York in the East" and "the Paris of the Orient". Besides, almost all of the heroic figures emerged in the modern history of China have left their footprints behind in this piece of land.

And now, encouraged by the instruction of late senior leader Deng Xiaoping, Shanghai has undergone a great change every three years in addition to having achieved a change every year. Then, with a tremendous success achieved in reform and development, this world-known metropolis has become now not only an international centre of economy, finance, trade and navigation on the western bank of the Pacific Ocean, but also an international tourist metropolis noted for its having an intriguing, unique blend of Chinese and Western influences. In short, Shanghai has turned itself into an open, fashion and dynamic metropolis. Just like magnolia denudata (the symbol flower of the city) in broom, Shannghai is full of life and vitality, and, at the same time, just as a pacemaker, it strides forward day and night in high spirits.

The scenic spots in Shanghai are really too many for the eye to take in. Built in different period of time and in various architectural style of the world, the grand complex of high-rise buildings on the either bank of Huangpu River is reputed as "the International Fair of World Architecture". On the eastern bank of the river, there are rows upon rows of high-rise structure dominating the skyline, including the Oriental TV Tower and the 88-storey Zenmao Building. Standing in the observation deck, you will soon have a clear panorama view of Shanghai's spectacular redevelopment over previous years. As the core part of this world-famous metropolis, there are many other attractive scenic spots, such as the People's Square, the Shanghai Museum, the Municipal Exhibition Hall of Shanghai Urban Construction and Shanghai Grand Theatre. However, despite of striving to accelerate the speed of modernization, the municipal administrations have paid much attention to the restoration and protection of many historical and cultural sites. For example, all of the sites, including the Yu Garden, the Site of the First Congress of CPC, the former residences of Mao Zedong, Dr. Sun Yat-sen, Madame Soong Ching-ling and Lu Xun have been restored and well protected. Besides, there are many fascinating scenic spots and resorts in the suburbs of Shanghai. As for the night scenes, with the successive accomplishment of the endeavours to beautify the city, Shanghai has also made a remarkable progress. As a result, with the accomplishment of many gigantic projects to beautify its appearance, Shanghai is now equal to compare favourably with any metropolis in the world.

Architecture is "the history of stone" and "the music in a condensed form". However, on this small piece of land there get together multifarious houses and urban facilities in different style, such as the residence in traditional Chinese style, the villa in the modern Western style and the newly-emerged communication facilities, including metros, light rails, ring road, flyover and expressways. So, just like a piece of musical symphony, each of its note is constutited to tell the process of this great urban construction. At present, the emergence of green space one after another in many part of this city shows clearly that Shanghai has made up its mind to make the city become beautiful more and more.

Reputed as "the shoppers' nirvana", Shanghai boasts many magnificent shopping malls, including the pedestrian street on Nanjing Road; the bustling Huaihai

Road, the Yu Garden Bazzar; the Xujiahui Shopping Centre; the 24-Hour Shopping Mall at Shanghai Railway Station and the New Century Shopping Centre in Pudong New Area. Each of these places is busy with people coming and going all the time. Hence, they have become now the favourite destinations for the tourists. As for the Shanghai Stock Exchange, there is always a mass of bobbing heads. The flashing eyes of its participants show vividly, however, the outstanding characteristics of Shanghainese known for their economy-mindedness and the spirit of hard struggle.

Although the rthym of the metropolitan life is quite fast, yet the residents' cultural activities are multifarious. While the traditional cultural activities have kept on their existence, many fashionable entertainments begin to appear one after another. Especially during the period of the Golden Tourism Week ( such as the Spring Festival, the May First and the National Day), a series of celebration activities will be arranged, including the Bell Toll Ceremony held to meet the arrival of New Year; the Temple Fair at Longhua; the Peachblossom Festival at Nanhui; the Shanghai International Tea Festival; the Shanghai Sweet-Scented Osmanthus Festival; the Shanghai Tourism Festival and the Shanghai International Film Festival. At that time, with the full demonstration of both folk customs and the folk art peculiar to Shanghai, you will have a good chance to enjoy the charm of Shanghai-style culture.

"To experience the gourmet's luck in Shanghai" --- Shanghai really lives up to this reputation. It is simply because there are a good number of restaurants noted for their authentic cousines in various style. For instance, apart from many foreign (such as Korean, Japanese and Western) food, there are dishes in various regional style, such as Shanghai, Yangzhou, Anhui, Hangzhou, Ningbo, Tianjin, Beijing, Wuxi, Cantoon, Sichuan, Fujian, Chaozhou, Hongkong, Macao and Taiwan. Besides, there are also a great lot of local delicacies. In a word, Shanghai deserves to be called "the Gourmet's Paradise".

To roam around this grand metropolis, it will bring you a great enjoyment as well as a refreshing excitement. And both of them are bound to give the same result: the vitality of life. Therefore, once in the face of world-known Huangpu River and Suzhou Creek, it is natural that the famous remark by Confucious (" Oh, time passes just like water in this river. It is flowing away unceasingly day and night.") will ring instantly in our mind and, instead of idling away our time, we must enjoy the present happiness in every quarter of our life.

3.金色的黄浦江
The glistening Huangpu River.

3

4.外滩，位于黄浦江畔，错落有致的西方古典建筑群，鳞次栉比，巍然矗立，是一个融合了斑斓历史和现代风采的观光胜地。

Located on the western bank of the Huangpu River, the Bund is lined with buildings in various European style. It is a world-known tourist destination where get together many cultural relics and scenic spots reflecting the history and the tremendous development of Shanghai.

# 东方明珠

在中国大陆南北海岸线的中心，在万里长江的入海口，镶嵌着一颗璀璨夺目的"东方明珠"，这就是繁华富丽的上海市。

上海，是中央直辖市，为中国最大的经济都会，以开放的海港城市特色、兼收并蓄的文化精神、灿若星辰的伟人胜迹以及中国共产党的诞生地而著称于世。1986年被国务院公布为国家历史文化名城。已跻身于世界十大城市之列。

上海，位于中国东部沿海、全国大陆海岸中部长江口南岸，地处长江三角洲前缘的河口三角洲上，襟江临海，水陆辉映，平畴沃野，河道纵横。黄浦江、吴淞江(苏州河)流贯市区，孕育了上海这座伟大的城市。上海辖区总面积6340.5平方公里，其中市区面积749平方公里。现辖16个区3个县，总人口1674万。居民以汉族为主。属北亚热带海洋性季风气候，年平均气温15.7℃，四季分明，温和湿润，为旅游营造了优良的气候条件。

上海，是中国重要的交通枢纽，水陆空交通，全方位、立体化、现代化，非常便捷。铁路有京沪、沪杭两条干线连接南北各线并延展至全国。公路纵横交错，四通八达。高速公路有京沪、沪嘉、莘松、沪宁、沪杭甬等联系全国各地。上海虹桥机场是中国主要的国际机场，有连接91个城市的国际国内航线300余条。上海浦东机场一期工程建成并投入运营，具有世界一流的先进设施。黄金水道长江，使上海的经济腹地从南京延伸到武汉、重庆直至金沙江流域，市区的黄浦江可通航2万多吨轮船。上海港是上海的经济命脉，现拥有万吨级码头泊位50个，下设10多个装卸区，1996年货物吞吐量达16402万吨，约占全国的1/3，是世界十大海港之一。海轮通沿海各大港口，国际海运可达五大洲160多个国家和

地区400多个港口。长江轮可直至四川重庆。内河航线沟通太湖流域，有内河航道240余条。上海市区内公共交通有各种车辆线路近千条。高架路有内环线和南北高架线，东西线延安路高架，外环线也已部分通车。地铁一号线从莘庄到上海火车站，并正向北延伸。二号线从中山公园到龙东路，并正向西延伸，尚有轻轨明珠一号线已通车，明珠二号线正在建设。以浦东龙阳路至浦东机场的上海磁悬游列车工程已正式启动。黄浦江上有对江轮渡12处、江底隧道2条、大桥5座(松浦、奉浦、徐浦、南浦、杨浦)，把浦东、浦西连成一体，形成珠联璧合的交通态势。

上海，既有数千年悠久而多彩的地区历史，又有710余年曲折而辉煌的建城历史。早在6000年前，上海的西部地区已经成为陆地，并出现了原始村落。这个时期被命名为马家浜文化。以后又经历了5000年前的崧泽文化和4000年前的良渚文化。这些远古文明序列，同北方西安半坡、河南渑池、泰安大汶口等处古代文明相辉映，共同创造了中华民族的远古历史。上海地区有文字可考的历史可以上溯到4000多年前的夏、商、周时代。在西周、春秋时，古木葱茏的上海西南部，成了贵族们飞鹰走犬的猎场。吴国寿梦王朝在这里建起了名为"华亭"的村镇，作为人、马停歇的场所，"华亭"就成了古上海的第一个名称。后来越国灭吴，楚国吞越，这一带就变成了楚国贵族春申君黄歇的封地，所以"申"或"春申"成了上海的简称或别称。

公元3世纪的西晋时代，吴淞江下游及其入海口处，已被命名为"沪渎"。《古图经》上就有"沿松江，下沪渎"的记载。公元4世纪初的东晋时代，在海岸线上又修建了防海要垒沪渎垒。"渎者，独也"，凡江河独流入海者为"渎"。"沪"者为一种竹编捕鱼工具。上海简称"沪"即由"沪渎"简化引申而来。从晋到宋末，"沪渎"之名整整用了10个世纪，这个称呼比上海之名要早500多年。同时也说明，至迟不会晚于东晋，上海地区已出现了渔民村落。

随着吴淞江下游渐渐淤积成陆，北宋天圣元年(公元1023年)已在上海浦岸(今外滩至十六

铺一带的黄浦江岸)设上海酒务，是文献记载的上海作为聚落名称之始。南宋景定至咸淳初年(公元1260～1267年)始在今市区建上海镇，并设市舶司。元至元二十八年(公元1291年)，元朝政府正式批准分设上海县，管辖华亭县东北和黄浦江东西两岸的5个乡，这在上海城市发展史上，具有里程碑的伟大意义。这时的浦江两岸已成市场繁盛、商舶云集之所，与泉州、广州齐名，成为当时海内外著名的开放港口城市。明清之际，上海地区棉纺织业空前发展，所产棉布，品质优良，远销关外、山陕、闽广以及南洋，有"衣被天下"之盛誉。明代，上海已发展成为"江海通津"、"东南都会"，呈现出"一城烟火半东南"的繁荣景象。鸦片战争后，1843年上海被迫开埠，1927年析上海县城区设上海特别市。1949年中华人民共和国成立后定为中央直辖市。1984年辟为对外开放城市，1993年成立浦东新区，扩大开放，从此上海步入了新的历史发展时期。

上海在中国近代史上占有重要的地位，并形成了独特的城市风格。鸦片战争以后，帝国主义列强强迫清政府开辟上海为商埠，历史上称作"开埠"，即开辟通商口岸。这次开埠是在帝国主义列强炮口下被迫开放的，充满了血泪和屈辱。但在另一方面，上海被迫开埠，帝国主义列强争相到此划定租界，经营工商业，并由此形成开放的港口城市特色。各国风格的经典建筑林立，被誉为万国建筑博物馆，成为重要的旅游资源。上海是移民城市，居民来自国内各地、世界各国，不同的文化在此交融碰撞，形成不拘陈规、敢于创新、兼收并蓄的"海派"风格。开埠以来，上海以它博大的胸怀，包容一大批叱咤风云的政治家、实业家和科学文化巨人，上海的文物古迹因此以名人遗迹为特色，孙中山故居、鲁迅故居、宋庆龄故居、周恩来公馆等保存完好。上海也是中国共产党的诞生地，1921年7月，中共第一次全国代表大会在此召开，宣告中国共产党成立。上海也因此而成为一个具有光荣革命传统和英雄本色的城市。上海最突出的风格与特点是工商业繁荣

昌盛，充满无限的生机与活力，是中国最大的工商业城市和经济中心，是中国改革开放、飞跃发展的前沿阵地。

上海是西太平洋地区重要的国际港口城市，中国对外开放的龙头城市。解放前，工业产品以消费资料为主。建国后已改建成为重、轻工业各个门类齐全的综合性工业基地。钢铁、机械、造船、仪表、电子、化学、纺织、医药、印刷等工业都在全国占有重要地位，形成了汽车、通信信息设备、钢铁、石油化工及精细化工加工、电站设备及配件和家用电子电器等六大支柱产业。建有宝山钢铁总厂、金山石油化工总厂等大型企业。工业总产值为51262亿元，以机械、冶金、化工为主导产业。上海商业繁荣，国内外贸易额居全国各大城市之首，2000年1722亿元，外贸出口总值约占全国的1/4。金融中心地位进一步突出，在伦敦、巴黎、纽约、新加坡、香港等国际金融中心设有联行。上海也是国内、国际通讯枢纽，全国对外通讯中，有1/3通过上海卫星地面站和中日海底电缆传输。上海教育科技综合实力位居全国前列。上海的城市布局，现以黄浦区为政治、金融、商业、文化中心；徐汇区是教育、科研、卫生机构集中地；普陀区为纺织、铸造工业区；杨浦区为纺织机械、冶金、造船工业区；宝山区是上海钢铁城；闵行区是上海机电工业城；浦东新区是蓬勃发展的高新技术产业区和国际经济合作区。上海的文化事业也很发达，上海大剧院是目前中国最好的剧院，上海图书馆的藏书仅次于国家图书馆。以商务旅行、都市观光为主的上海旅游业正在兴起并蓬勃发展。上海现已成为中国最大的经济、金融、贸易、航运中心，也是国际经济、金融、贸易、航运中心之一。

5～6.东方明珠广播电视塔是今日上海的标志性建筑。

The Dazzling Pearl of the Orient.

## The Dazzling Pearl of the Orient

Located in the middle of China's coastline, Shanghai is a world-known metropolis in China. Reputed as a dazzling pearl of the Orient, it is inlaid on the place where the Yangtze River empties itself into the East China Sea.

As one of the four municipalities directly under the central government, Shanghai is the most prosperous commercial city in China. Famous for its open to the outside world and rich in social and tourist resources, Shanghai is approved by the State Council as a top-level historical and cultural city in the country and, what's more, it has been long ranked as one the ten grand metropolis in the world.

Close to the end of the mighty Yangtze River, where the fertilized land is known as "the rich Yangtze delta", Shanghai is, therefore, endowed with excellent natural conditions. The city occupies a total of 6,340.5 square kilometres, of which the urban area is 749 square kilometres. With 16 districts and 3 counties under its jurisdiction, it has a population of 16,740,000, of which Han nationality is the main part. Situated in the subtropical zone, Shanghai enjoys the annual average temperature 15.7°c. As a result, with a clear distinction between the four seasons, the city has become more and more appealing to tourists from both home and abroad.

Besides, Shanghai is also one of the important, 3-D, all-direction and modernized hubs in China, it boasts a convenient communication in the field of water, air and land transportation. In terms of the land transportation, there are Beijing-Shanghai and Hangzhou-Shanghai railway key routes, which, apart from linking all of the other railway routes, have extended to any part of the country. As for the highway, Shanghai features a complete system, leading to every part of the country through its key expressways, including Shanghai-Jiaxing; Shanghai-Nanjing and Shanghai-Hangzhou. In terms of air transportation,the Hongqiao Airport in Shanghai is one of China's major international air-ports, it boasts of having opened 300-odd international and domestic routes,

leading to 91 cities all over the world. Besides, the Pudong International Airport boasts of having many first-grade advanved facilities in the world, and it has begun to operate soon after the completion of its first stage construction. As a busy hub of coastal shipping, Shanghai connects China's inland areas (including Nanjing, Wuhan and Chongqing) via the navigation routes along the Yangtze River. Shanghai handels a third of China's seagoing freight (in excess of 164 million tons in 1996). There are 50 berths and more than 10 container terminals in the port. As one of the world's ten largest ports, Shangia's seagoing freight reaches to about 400 seaports in more than 400 countries and regions throughout the world. A newly-completed modern seaway allows ships about 20,000 tons to enter the Huangpu River. As for the inland navigation, the city serves more than 240 routes, connecting all of the ports along the Taihu Lake area. With the accomplishment of major infrastructure projects, including new inner ring road, elevated highways and numerous flyovers, the problem of traffic jams has long been solved. Shanghai buses offer convenient service throughout the city. Running from the Xinzhuang in the south to the Railway Station in the north, No. 1 Metro Line has long been completed, while No. 2 Metro Line is scheduled to extend as far as to the end of the western suburbs. Meanwhile, the light rails, Pearl No. 1 and Pearl No.2 are under construction. Besides, acesses to the Pudong New Area across the Huangpu River has been fascilitated by the completion of five magnificent bridges (including Songpu, Fengpu, Xupu, Nanpu and Yangpu) in addition to 12 ferries and two underground tunnels. Running from Longyang Road to Pudong Airport, a brand-new light rail is being scheduled.

Built on the basis of an accumulation of local culture for several decades of centuries, Shanghai enjoys a history of more than seven hundred years. As early as six thousand years before, the western part of Shanghai had long become a land and, what's more, began to emerge on it a primitive village. According to the estimation made by archaeologists, it was called Majiabang culture. Later on, this

place had further undergone the following two stages of development: the Songze Culture (5,000 years ago) and the Liangzhu culture (4,000 years ago). Together with the Banpo in Xi'an and the Dawenkou in Tai'an, they have formed a long and glorious history of the Chinese nation.

In tracing the history of Shanghai, one will certainly not miss the County of Songjiang some 40 kilometers southwest of the urban area.At the time of the Warring States (475-221 B.C.), this ancient city with a history of over 2,000 years was built originally as a sumptuous pavilion to greet the King of Wu during his trip of hunting. So, Huating (a sumptuous pavilion) had become the first name of ancient Shanghai. Before long, with Huating's being occupied by the State of Chu, the land had become a fief of Prince Chun Shen, prime minister to the King of the State of Chu. As a result, Shanghai is also sometimes known as Chunshen or Shen for short.

During the Western Jin Dynasty (265-316), Shanghai had turned itself into a fishing village. Hence, when the Chinese want to be literary, or brief, they call Shanghai "Hu". The name bespeaks Shanghai's origins as a fishing village, for *Hu* is a bamboo fishing device used during the third century by the people who lived around the Songjiang River. Later on, with the appearance of a fertilized land at the mouth of Yangtze River, a township sprang into being on the western bank of Songjiang River (subsequently renamed Wusong River). Endowed with many natural advantages, the place had become a busy port with many junks and ships coming to berth. In the first year of the reign of Tiansheng (1023) during the Northern Song Dynasty (960-1127), a tax office was set up in Shanghai. In the 28th year of the reign of Zhiyuan during the Yuan Dynasty (1291), Shanghai and four other towns in Huating were brought together to form the County of Shanghai. Before long, since the rapid development of textile industry, Shanghai gained the fame of "its production of clothes being on sale everywhere". By the time of the Ming Dynasty (1368-1644), with the backing of its port, Shanghai began to flourish, enjoying widespread renown as "a bustling port,, and "a grand metropolis in the Southeast,,. After the Opium Wars in 1843, Shanghai was forced to agree to an open trade port. In 1927, Shanghai became a special municipality under the Kuomingtang regime. After the founding of People's Republic of China in 1949, Shanghai became one of the municipalities directly under the Central Government. In 1984, Shanghai was approved as an opened-up city and, nine years later, New Pudong Area was established. Ever since then Shanghai has enjoyed a new lease of life.

As a city with unique feature, Shanghai occupies an important position in the modern history of China. After the Opium Wars in 1843, under the meance of gun-fire by the Western powers, the Qing-dynasty government was forced to agree to the opening of Shanghai as a Treaty port. Then, with the struggles between these Western powers, there began to appear a couple of the International Settlements in Shanghai. In such a case, with the boom of commerce and industry under their administration, Shanghai had obtained an extraordinary feature. As a matter of fact, Shanghai is a melting point. Even many of the Shanghai natives had originally come from somewhere else. There grew up in Shanghai a class of people who were brave to absorb another culture without the debasement of their own. In this way, ever since its establishment, Shanghai has attracted a good number of talented politicians, enterprenuers as well as giants in scientific and literary circles. Meanwhile, the city has thus become rich in relics. For instance, there are many well-preserved former residences of the celebrities, such as Dr. Sun Yat-sen, Lu Xun, Madame Soong Ching-ling and the late premier Zhou Enlai. Besides, it is also the birthplace of the Communist Party of China. So, it is natural that Shanghai is a city endowed with glorious tradition of revolution and the fighting spirit of heroes. In a word, noted for its open-up minded and exploring spirit, Shanghai is China's largest centre of commerce, trade and economy. It stands nowadays in the fore front of China's reform and development.

Apart from being one of the important international port cities in the westrn Pacific area, Shanghai is the "Dragon Head,, city of China in the field of opening up to the outside world. Before the liberation in 1949, the major industrial products in Shanghai were mainly consumer goods. However, soon after the founding of the People's Republic of China, the place was turned into an industrial base covering many heavy and light industries, such as iron, steel, machinery, ship-building, instrument, electronic, chemistry, textile, medicine and printing. And, furthermore, they all have occupied an important position in the total output of the country. As a resul, with the establishment of many large-scale enterprises, including Baoshan Iron & Steel Works snd Jinshan Petro-Chemical Works, the following six pillar industries are formed now in Shanghai: automobile, telecommunications, steel, power station equipment, fine petrochemicals and home electric appliances. With machinery, iron-melting and chemical as its major industries, the total industrial output value has reached 5,126,200 million yuan. Meanwhile, the commerce is quite prosperous in Shanghai, the total amount of both domestic and foreign trade in this city reached 172,200 million yuan in the year of 2000, which ranks first among the large cities across the country. Besides, Shanghai's total value of exports accounts for one fourth of the whole country. With establishment of the branches of our financial institutions in London, Paris, New York, Singarpore and Hongkong, the city's position as an international financial centre is further secured. Since one third of the worldwide telecommunications practised in the country is accomplished through the transmition by the Shanghai Satellite Ground Station and the Sino-Japanese Sea-Bottom Electric Lines, Shanghai also ranks first as far as the comprehensive force of education and science is concerned. As for the industrial structure, the city authorities have made such a wise arrangement: Huangpu District strives to become the centre of politics, finance, commerce and culture; Xuhui District is aimed to become a concentrated place for the institutions of education, science, and hygiene;

Pudu District—the industrial area of textile and foundry ; Yangpu District—the industrial area of textile machinery, metallurgy and ship-building; Baoshan District—the Iron and Steel Town of Shanghai; Mingheng District—the industrial town of electric machinery; the Pudong New Area—the booming area of high and new techinology sector as well as the international economic cooperation. The cultural undertaking in Shanghai is quite prosperous as well. For instance, the Shanghai Grand Theatre is acclaimed as the most magnificent one in China. The total collection of the Shanghai Library is second to that of the National Library of China in Beijing. With its major in business trip and metroplis sightseeing, the tourism in Shanghai has not only risen up, but also made a rapid development. And now, apart from being the largest centre of economy, finance, trade, and navigation in China, Shanghai has become one of the important international centres of economy, finance, trade and navigation in the world.

7.三年巨变的上海浦东开发区
Pudong New Area has undergone a great change in three years.

7

# 旅游风光

　　上海，既是中国历史文化名城，又是中国首屈一指的现代化大都市，拥有丰富的人文资源、迷人的城市风貌、繁华的商业街市、中西交汇的民族风情和欢乐的节庆活动，形成了上海独特的都市旅游风光，使上海成为一座融古色古香和现代潮流为一体的旅游中心城市。上海市共有13处全国重点文物保护单位、113处市级文物保护单位，175处近代优秀建筑，每一处都凝聚并展示了鲜明的"海派"文化特色。上海市拥有300多个游览点，内容丰富，门类齐全，多姿多彩。其中名胜古迹有豫园、玉佛寺、龙华塔、松江唐经幢等；都市风貌有外滩景区、浦东新景区、人民广场、上海著名商城商街，如南京路等；自然风光有黄浦江、淀山湖、佘山国家森林公园、东平国家森林公园等；革命遗址有中共"一大"会址、名人故居和陵墓；还有城市规划展示馆、少年宫、博物馆、图书馆、大剧院、科技城、青少年活动基地和大型乐园等。

　　黄浦江两岸雄伟壮丽的人文景观，集中体现了上海大都市的繁华风貌。浦西外滩景区和浦东新景区活像两条巨大而又悠长的立体画廊，展现在浦江两岸的广阔天地之间。

　　上海外滩，是上海的象征，为中外游客必到之处。外滩，北起外白渡桥，沿宽阔的中山东一路往南，直抵延安东路，全长1700米，其间点缀着绿地、花草、雕塑、喷泉。沿江岸线向江心方向外移了6米至49米，并筑有高6.9米、宽14.4米的防汛墙。上层平台沿江有栏杆，供游人观赏江景。平台下有一层花坛、喷水池、绿化带，下面是人行道。在南京路外滩塑陈毅铜像，福州路口有人物浮雕群，黄浦公园东北隅建有人民英雄纪念塔。中山东一路由原来的6个车道拓宽到现在37米宽的10个车道，车速每小时可达50公

16

8.流光溢彩的外滩夜色，是上海都市旅游的重要标志景区之一。

The night scene on the Bund is one of the important landmarks of Shanghai's tourisum sector.

里。外滩经二期工程改建后，从延安东路延伸至南浦大桥，全长2860米。整个外滩一气呵成，变得更加美丽动人。宽阔悠长的外滩，面对百舸争流的黄浦江，背倚52幢接天连云、风格不同的建筑群，构成水陆相映的近代世界建筑博览会。站在外滩滨江大道上，凭栏远眺，江面上大大小小船舶穿梭不息，轮船欢快的汽笛声和黄浦江水拍岸涛声优美动听。浦江游览已成为上海的特色旅游之一。游览从新外滩码头起航出发，将您从繁华热闹的市区，带到烟波浩淼的长江入海口。外滩，呈现出一派繁忙景象。早上，这里是市民晨练散步的好地方；白天是国内外游客观光游览的天地；晚上则是对对情侣谈情说爱的理想场所；每逢周末和节日，这里充满欢歌笑语。对生活充满了激情的中外团体和艺术家们汇集在陈毅元帅塑像前的广场上，吹拉弹唱，引吭高歌，艺贯中西、古今，构成了沪上广场文化的又一新景。夜幕降临，华灯初上，数十幢大厦披上了一件件绚丽的光纱，灯光点面结合，动静相宜，色彩亮丽，气势辉煌，如一座座晶莹剔透的水上宫殿。临江远眺整个外滩建筑群，璀璨夺目，豪华壮观。高楼上灯光灿烂，高楼流光如潮，参差跌宕，气势非凡，艳丽绝世。

　　站在上海外滩，透过夜幕，隔江遥看对岸，风光旖旎的"东方明珠"和陆家嘴新兴金融贸易中心建筑群的各色灯光一片灿烂，浮映在金波粼粼的江面上，这就是浦东新景区的光辉形象。浦东新区面积522.8平方公里，具有很强的地理优势和良好的开发条件。短短几年时间，在浦东的大地上，东方明珠广播电视塔、金茂大厦、杨浦大桥、南浦大桥、奉浦大桥、徐浦大桥、松浦大桥、内环线高架浦东段、上海环球金融中心、浦东国际机场、滨江大道、世纪大道等现代化建筑如雨后春笋破地而现。由中央公园、陆家嘴金融贸易区、金桥出口加工区、外高桥保税区、张江高科技园区、华夏文化旅游区、孙桥现代农业园区等构成的新区现代化都市景观纷纷建成，浦东新区正在向多功能的现代化、国际化的目标快步前进。

　　东方明珠电视塔，位于浦东新区陆家嘴的

9. 繁花似锦上海滩
Shanghai—Growing attractive with each passing day.

10. 外滩建筑
The buildings along the Bund.

11. 人民英雄纪念塔
The Monument to the Heroes of People.

12. 外滩雕塑墙
The sculpture wall on the Bund.

黄浦江边，高度仅次于加拿大多伦多电视塔和俄罗斯莫斯科奥斯坦金电视塔，位居亚洲第一、世界第三。该塔1991年动工，1994年建成，高468米，占地55000平方米，建筑面积79000平方米。以3根直径7米的钢柱斜撑3根直径9米的擎天柱。在90米、236米和350米处，各有直径50米、45米、14米的3个球型塔。塔之底部为2000平方米的门厅，厅有4层，地面地下各2层，设置展览厅、录像厅和商场。塔座内还设有科幻城和上海历史博物馆。有7部电梯从擎天柱内升入第一个球，球内分8层，主厅内有商店、娱乐厅、摄影厅。乘电梯进入236米的第二球中只需40秒钟时间。走近玻璃墙壁，环顾四周，上海市景尽收眼底：黄浦江如玉带展开，蜿蜒入海，巨轮如梭，往来不断。横跨于江上的南浦大桥和杨浦大桥似两条巨龙腾空而起，与中间的东方明珠塔遥相呼应，如二龙戏珠。入夜，浦江如画，由计算机控制的缤纷彩灯悄然亮起，灯光可根据天气自动调节，产生上千种变化。远观塔身，如一串巨大、耀眼的夜明珠，悬于半空，与群星争辉，与江对岸外滩的灯光建筑群竞相媲美，展现出上海迷人的大都市之夜景。在236米的观光层可乘电梯从单根空筒升至350米小型球体内，被称为太空舱，为贵宾观光处。该塔于1995年对外开放，每天可容6000人次登塔。此塔与扩大至15.5万平方米的浦东公园融为一体，三根斜柱体上的三个球体，和大中小三个球体，以及空中旅馆五个球体、平地上四个球体，共十五个球体，构成"大珠小珠落玉盘"的意境，故有"东方明珠"之称，是上海的标志性建筑。

金茂大厦耸立于黄浦江畔陆家嘴金融贸易区中心，遥对东方明珠广播电视台，毗邻延安东路隧道口，与地铁二号线连通。大厦高420.5米，其主体建筑地上88层，地下3层，占地面积23611平方米，总建筑面积29万平方米。它是上海迈向21世纪的标志性建筑之一，其高度仅次于马来西亚吉隆坡的双塔大厦和美国芝加哥的西尔斯大厦，是目前国内第一，世界第三高楼，是东方塔形建筑风格与现代科学技术完美结合的超高层摩天大楼。它创造了我国建筑"高、精、深、新"

13. 设施一流、馆藏极丰富的上海博物馆，以收藏青铜器、陶瓷、书画珍品著称，藏品达13万余件。

Accommodated with the most advanced facilities, the Shanghai Museum boasts a total of more than 130 thousand items of relics, including bronze, ceramics, paintings and sculptures.

14. 上海大剧院的建筑设计和设备配置，达到了世界一流水平。

The design and facility of the Shanghai Grand Theatre have attained the top level throughout the world.

15. 人民广场是上海的公共活动中心，也是浦西市区的巨大"绿肺"。

The People's Square is a public activity centre in Shanghai and it is also functioned as a "green lug,, of Shanghai's western area.

16. 人民广场
People's Square.

21

等方面的新纪录,与东方明珠塔堪称我国现代建筑的"双绝"。金茂大厦是融办公、商务、宾馆等多功能为一体的智能化高档楼宇。距地面341米的第88层为国内迄今最高的观光层。高速电梯45秒钟可将观光宾客从地下室一层直接送达观光层。此外,浦东新区的滨江大道集防汛墙体、江边大道、亲水平台、音乐喷泉、游艇码头于一体,被称为浦东的"新外滩"。一期工程南起东昌轮渡码头,沿浦江东岸"东方明珠"至泰同栈码头,全长1500米,在"东方明珠"与富都世界之间架起连接天桥,成为一道亮丽的风景线。

豫园,是上海古典园林的杰出代表,为全国重点文物保护单位,被誉为"奇秀甲于江南",素有"城市山林"之美称。豫园位于黄浦区城隍庙的东北面,是上海现存的一所最完整的明代园林,建造于明嘉靖三十八年(公元1559年),至万历五年(公元1577年)。后陆续扩建达4.7公顷。原为明代四川布政司潘允端的私人花园,取"豫(通愉)悦老亲"之意,故名。其园林布局虚实互映,大小对比,高低相称,前呼后应,曲折有法,充分体现了园林艺术的特色,再缀以亭台楼阁、大池溪流、奇峰异石、嘉树秀木,更显得妩媚多姿。尤其是明代著名园艺家张南阳的叠石假山,把园林艺术推向了崭新的境界。

豫园分内外两园,以外园为主体。园内共有5条浸透着精灵秀气的巨龙装饰围墙,誉称龙墙。全园40余处景观被这栩栩如生的龙墙、蜿蜒曲折的回廊以及形状各异的花草巧妙地分隔成6个景区,形成一步一景、步移景换的艺术美境。园中的大假山是明代所遗的惟一真品,是用浙江武康黄石堆叠而成,为累石名家张南阳的精心杰作。假山高仅12米,远远望去,却显得雄伟壮观,气势磅礴;深谷幽壑,连绵起伏;清泉飞瀑,画意盎然,具有以小见大的艺术特色。玉华堂正前有3座亭亭玉立的石峰,中间一座是玉玲珑,高3.3米,石上有72个孔洞相通,具有"漏、空、绉、瘦、透"之美,传为宋代花石纲遗物,与苏州留园冠云峰、杭州花圃掇景园内的绉云峰、南京瞻园的仙人峰合称为江南四大名石。有趣的

22

17.上海城市规划展示馆

The Exhibition Hall of the Shanghai Urban Construction.

18.大世界游乐中心创办于1917年，是上海最早出现的一个大型综合性游乐场。内设电影院、桌球室、舞厅、溜冰场、游艺宫等。雅俗共赏，深受游客欢迎。

Built in 1937 and renovated in 1949, the Great World, one of the earliest recreation centres in Shanghai, contains now a cinema, a dance room, a roller-skating rink and other recreational facilities. It is wellreceived by both the locals and tourists.

19.杂技表演

An acrobatic performance.

20.人民公园，昔日的赌场跑马厅，1951年改建为闹中取静的休憩场所。

Laid out in 1951 on what used to be the British-run racecourse, Peple's Square is a 12-hectare oasis of trees, pool and decorative rocks. It has become now a plesant rest place in the downtown area.

是，在玉玲珑下面烧一炷香，上面会孔孔冒烟；上面浇一盆水，下面又会洞洞流泉，泉水齐涌，蔚为奇观。

豫园内万花楼东的点春堂是豫园的建筑精华，堂名取苏东坡"翠点春妍"之意。该堂曾为1853年上海小刀会起义的城北指挥所。凤舞鸾吟是点春堂对面的小对台，背临水池，式样新巧。有一座听鹤亭，上有题云："柳梢听得黄鹂语，此是春来第一声。"诗句和翠点春妍相联系，构成一幅有声有色的山水画图。豫园的园中之园——内园在豫园东南部，面积仅1200多平方米，亭台楼阁兼容，山川湖泊并蓄，树木花卉，疏密有致，具有我国造园艺术之特色。九龙池壁刻有4条小龙，造型栩栩如生。园南辟有豫园曲苑，有光绪年间所建之戏台，顶部藻井精雕细琢，枋上镌刻故事画，金碧辉煌，经常有昆剧、京剧演出，为上海一座古典剧场。"不游豫园，不算到上海"，这是中外旅游者的共同心声。

豫园与南翔的古猗园、嘉定的秋霞圃、青浦的曲水园、松江的醉白池，合称沪城五大古典名园，被誉为园林中的五朵金花。古猗园的布局具有苏州园林的特色，水面面积较大，蜿蜒环绕全园。以戏鹅池为中心，西南又辟大池。亭台楼阁散立池畔，意境深远。珍贵文物较多，素享盛名。园内的两座唐经幢，是南翔寺遗物，雕刻精致，造型优美。秋霞圃布局以水池居中心。池南假山以土带石，山坞曲径，林木参天，亭轩阁榭多隐于山石花墙之间；北部黄石假山，有洞壑峭壁之胜，其厅堂布置较为显露，形成了明暗对比的造园艺术特色。醉白池，以池水为主，环池三面皆曲廊亭榭，晴雨均可凭栏赏景，饶有幽旷意趣。曲水园景以大假山和荷花池为中心，山石、水体、花木配置合宜，构成水随山转、山因水活、绿荫繁茂的江南水乡景色。园内花木扶疏，古树尤多，其中有棵罗汉松与凌霄交缠在一起，凌霄花开犹如松树生花，别成一景，有"松舞凌霄"之美称。

在上海众多的人文景观中，堪与园林艺术相媲美的是寺庙建筑，玉佛寺是其中的佼佼者。玉佛寺殿宇仿宋代建筑，黄粉墙垣，飞檐耸脊，

21.浦东民俗博物馆
The Folk Custom Museum in Pudong.

22.位于东方明珠塔内的上海历史发展陈列馆,讲述了上海滩的变迁史。
　　Laid out in the Orient Pearl Tower, the Exhibition Hall of the Shanghai's Development features a brief history of Shanghai.

23.滨江大道
The Riverside Avenue.

24.黄浦江和浦东开发区
The Huaugpu River and the Pudong Developmnet Area.

照壁高大。主要建筑有天王殿、大雄宝殿、玉佛楼、卧佛堂。玉佛楼正中供玉佛坐像一尊，用整块白玉雕成，高约1.9米，重约1吨，身上佩戴着无数玛瑙翡翠宝石，实为稀世珍品。玉佛坐像，造型美观，色泽晶莹，神态端庄。卧佛堂中对面法物流通处供玉雕释迦牟尼涅槃像，亦用整块白玉雕成，长1米，神态自然逼真。徐汇区龙华镇的龙华塔建于三国吴大帝（孙权）赤乌年间（公元238年～250年），现塔基、塔身为宋代建筑，砖木结构，七级八面，高40.64米，各层飞檐高翘，栏杆曲折，外形雄伟美观。七层顶上有塔刹，高达8米，使宝塔越发显得绰约多姿。松江县唐经幢建于唐大中十三年（公元871年），是全国重点文物保护单位，为上海地区现存最完整的珍贵石刻艺术精品，也是上海最古的地面建筑。这座经幢是用大青石雕刻垒砌而成，现存21级，高9.3米，幢身八面，上下各级均有雕刻，层层石雕，花团锦簇，疏密有间，丰富多彩，富于变化。雕刻精致细腻，技法洗练纯熟，充分显示了盛唐时期的艺术风格。松江宋方塔，原名兴圣教寺塔。也系全国重点文物保护单位。虽经历代修葺，仍保持宋代原貌，斗拱大部分保留宋代原物，是江南古塔中保留原有构件较多的一座古塔。砖木结构，九级方形，高42.5米，造型奇特优美，姿态玲珑可爱，具有我国南方宝塔挑檐窜角、清秀挺拔的艺术风格。松江明刻照壁，面阔3间，中间高4.75米，阔6.1米，上为巨幅雕刻怪兽"犭贪"，妄想吞吃旭日，被淹死海中。砖刻线条遒劲细致，画面生动，内容丰富，发人深思。松江天马山中峰上的护珠塔，高18米，侧向东南，倾斜度30°，超过意大利的比萨斜塔，成为一大奇观。

25.环境优美的浦东陆家嘴金融贸易区中心绿地
The green space at the centre of Lujiazhui Finace and Trade Zone in Pudong.

26.浦东国际机场夜色
The night scene at the Pudong Interational Airport.

27.国际会议中心
The International Convention Centre.

28.29.国际会议中心的地球厅，从里向外观赏景色，别有一番情趣。
The Globe Hall in the Shanghai International Convention Centre.

27

## Metropolitan Looks

Apart from being a well-known historical and cultural city in China, Shanghai is the leading modernized metropolis of this great country. It is endowed with abundant social and cultural resources, bustling shopping centres, colourful customs in various flavor and many exciting festival activities. Hence, Shanghai has become now a distinguished tourist destinction. With a total of 13 historical relics under the state protection, 113 sites under the municipal protection and 175 outstanding modren building erected over the previous years, they are most characteristic of Shanghai's regional culture. There are more than 300 scenic spots in Shanghai and, what's more, they are not only rich in category, but full of colouful content. For instance, in the field of historical sites and scenic spots, there are as follows: the Yu Garden, the Jade Buddha Temple, the Longhua Pagoda and the Tang-dynasty Sutra Tower in Songjiang. As for the metropolitan looks, there are: the scenic area in the Bund; the new scenic area in Pudong; the People's Square; the famous shopping malls on the Nanjing Road and the Huaihai Road. As for the natural scenic areas, there are: the Huangpu River; the Dianshan Lake; the Sheshan Forest Park and the National Forest Park in Dongping. In the field of the sites with revolutionary significance, there are: the site of the First Congress of CPC and others. Besides, there are also many worth-seeing places, including the former residence of celebrities, such as Dr. Sun Yat-sen and Madam Soong Ching-Ling; the Exhibition Hall of the Urban Construction; pioneers' palaces, museums, libraries, grand theatres, technology and science centre and the large-scale pleasure grounds.

As one of the outstanding representative of the structures built in classical Chinese style, Yu Garden, which lies to the north behind high walls in the Old Town, is one of the national-level relics under the state protection. A fully restored classical Chinese garden, it is similar to many of the famous gardens in Suzhou. Built by a Ming official, Pan Yunduan, for his father, the coustruction of this garden was completed in 1537.

28

31

32

### 30.浦东世纪公园
The Century Park in Pudong New Area.

### 31.金茂大厦高420.5米，是目前国内第一、世界第三高楼，也是上海迈向21世纪的标志性建筑之一。
The 420.5-metre-high Zenmao Building, the highest in China and the third in the world. It is regarded as a symbol of Shanghai's marching toward the 21st ceuntry.

### 32.浦东新区内的鹤鸣楼
Heming (Crane's Singing)Hall is located in the Pudong New Area.

### 33.上海太阳岛高尔夫球场
The Sun-Island Golf Court.

### 34.上海科技馆
Shanghai Scince and Technology Museum.

For many Chinese, gardens were a microcosm in which the skiful gardener could construct his own world using minerals, plants and animals in a confined space. Alhough the Yu Garden occupies less than two hectares (five acres), it seems far larger. The garden demonstrates perfectly the sophisticated art of combining several different elements to create a world in miniature—ingeniously mingling pavilions and corridors, small hills and carefully selected and placed rocks, lotus ponds with goldfish swimming in them, bridges, winding paths, trees and shrubs.

There are many details in the garden to look out for. Each section is divided up by white curving walls which are topped by the undulating body of a dragon. The walls end with splendidly carved dragon-heads. There are fine examples of the type of carved bricks found in Suzhou's gardens—earthenware pictures of animals, flowers or scenes illustrating legends. Many shapes and designs of ornamental windows—square, round, rectangular and polygonal—can be seen, with highly complicated lattice-work patterns.

"No visit to Shanghai is completed without a tour of the Yu Garden.,, It is the common voice made by the tourists from both home and abroad.

Apart from Yu Garden in the downtown of Shanghai, there are Guyi Garden in Nanxiang, Qiuxia Garden in Jiading, Qushui Garden in Qingpu and Zuibai Pool in Songjiang. They are acclaimed as the Five Golden Flowers in the field of Chinese architecture. Situated in Nanxiang Town, Jiading County, Guyi Garden was built in the Ming Dynasty and renovated in the Qing Dynasty. It is noted for its having preserved many cultural relics, such as the Tang-dynasty *jingchuang* (a stone pillar inscribed with Buddhist scriptures) and the ruins of Nanxiang Temple. Located in Jiading County, Qiuxia (Autumn Glow) Garden was formerly the private garden of Gong Hong, a Minister of War in the Ming Dynasty. It was built in the reigns of Zhende and Jiajing (1506-1522) and the designer ingeniously interspersed pavilions, towers and hills among rockeries, trees and ponds, resulting

35

36

30

35.流光溢彩的外滩之夜
The colouful night scene of thc Bund.

36.浦江两岸华灯初上
    The evening light on the either side of the
Huangpu River in Shanghai.

37.上海火车站周围已发展成为不夜城商业中心
    The 24-hour Shanghai Railway Station
Bazzar.

38.博物馆夜色
 The night scene of Shanghai Museum.

in a colourful and interdependent whole. The garden looks like a paradise under the rosy glow of autumn. Laid out in Songjiang County, Zuibai (Drunk Bai's Pool) was built in memory of Bai Juyi (772-846), a famous poet of the Tang Dynasty, who had come to stay here in his later years. Situated on the shore of Daying Lake in the northeastern corner of the Nanxiang countyseat. Qushui Garden (the Garden of Meandering Stream) is noted for several scenic spots, which have basically preserved the style and features of the old garden completed in 1745 during the reign of Emperor Qianlong in the Qing Dynasty.

Besides the classical gardens, there are many magnificent temples in Shanghai. As one of the most famous temples, the Jade Buddha Temple is noted for a 1.9 metre-high jade statue of Sakyamuni ; it was brought to the temple by the monk Huigen from Myanmar around 1876. Built according to the style popular during the Song Dynasty, it stands in the northwest of the city. The temple walls and the enormous gilded wooden statues have been repainted in bright colours.

Situated in the southwestern suburbs of Shanghai, Longhua Temple is famous for its ancient temple and pagoda. It is said the temple was built during the Three Kingdoms period (220-280). The seven-storey octagonal Longhua Pagoda is built of bricks and timber. Erected in 859, the Tang-dynasty Stone Pillar, 9.3 metres high and inscribed with Buddhist scriptures, is regarded as one of the key relics under the state protection.

A 48.5-meter-high nine-stage Square Pagoda is erecting in the city and, like a landmark, it reminds the people of the past glory of the ancient city. Built during 1068-1094, it is a rarely seen brick pagoda in the style of wooden pagoda of the Song dynasty, being a typical example of the evolution of pagoda structure of the Tang and the Song dynasties. The Screen Wall in front of the pagoda was built in 1370 (the 3rd year of the reign of Hongwu in the Ming dynasty). The screen is decorated with a massive brick bas-relief, 6 metres long and 4.5 metres across, which depicts an impossing legendary beast called Tan (Greedy). Trying to eat everything

39.上海体育场可容纳8万多名观众
The Shanghai Stadium has a seating capacilty of 80 thousand audiences.

40.外滩倒影
An inverted reflection of the Bund.

41.陆家嘴金融开发区
The Lujiazui Financial Development Area.

42.上海图书馆新馆
The new site of the Shanghai Library.

on earth, the "monster of avarice,, finally drowned by rushing into the sea to swallow it up. The exquisite screen warns every passer-by that greediness is insatiable and insatiability will lead to destruction. Located on the top of Tianma Hill, the Huzhu (Pearl-Protecting) Pagoda is also a precious relics. Standing there in a tilted manner, it looks just like the famous leaning tower of Pisa in Italy.

The Bund is the symbol of Shanghai and it is also a must for all of the visitors to Shanghai. Bounded on the east by the Huangpu River, a wide avenue curves along the western bank of the Huangpu River, dominated on one side by an imposing line of buildings in the grand European style. This impressive avenue is none other than the famous Bund, probably the best-known of all streeets in the East.

Acclaimed as the symbol of Shanghai, the Bund (called *Waitan* by the Chinese) is located on the west bank of the Huangpu River, where appears along the bank a line of high buildings in different style.

When evening comes, the banks of the Huangpu River are thronged with strolling young couples. In the early morning everyday, it is a good place for people to do their morning exercise, such as shadow boxer and the old man disco. In the evening, however, with the colourful light illuminating from the high buildings on either side of the Huangpu River, the whole place will soon look just as a dazzling palace in the night.

Huangpu Cruise, a 60-kilometre return trip between the Bund and Wusongkou (the mouth of Yangtze River), is the must for the first-time tourists to Shanghai. During this trip, you will enjoy a series of scenic spots including Fuxing Islet and the Wusong Fort.

The road runnig along the Bund is still as busy as ever—and it is now a vital link in the city's new highway network. Pedestrians are now forced underground through subways to emerge on a new elevated walkway along the waterfront.

As one of the city government's key projects for the 1990s, on which work is still continuing, the level of the promenade on the Bund has been raised to prevent possible flooding. Like Venice, Shanghai is slowly sinking. The imperative of raising the Bund

43

44

34

43.豫园，明嘉靖三十八年（公元1559年）兴建。园主潘允端，上海人，以"豫悦老亲"为其父养老建造的，故名。园内亭台楼阁、曲廊回环，保持了明、清建筑特色，为江南名园之一。

Built in the 38th year of the reign of Emperor Jiaqing (1559) during the Ming Dynsty, the Yu Garden was built by Pan Yunduan (a high officil) for his father. Containing many pavillions, corridors and structures in the style of the Ming and Qing Dynasties, it is ranked as one of the famous gardens in China.

44.豫园的金鱼池
A golden fish pool in the Yu Garden.

45.造型别致的仰山堂，登楼观望，可见一池相隔的假山。

Yangshan Tang (Hall for Viewing the Grand Rockery) is a beautiful two-storey structure on which one could appreciate the Grand Rockery across the pond.

45.豫园夜色
A night view of the Yu Garden.

has resulted in a wide, well-trodden path for visitors and pleasure-seekers, picture-snapping or relaxing in front of the busy harbour. On the site of the Huangpu Park, where the Huangpu River converges with Suzhou Creek, now stands a granite monument to the people's heroes.

Pudong, the city of the future, lies on the other side of the Huangpu River to the old International Settlement. The cityscape of Pudong is dominated by the 468-metre-high Shanghai Oriental TV Tower. The love-it-or-hate-it pinnacle has viewing areas for spectacular panoramas of the harbour, the old city areas and the Riverside Avenue's new landscaped riverfront terraces along the eastern bank of the Huangpu River.

Pudong New Area, the new landmark of Shanghai, lies on the other side of the Huangpu River to the Bund. Covering a total area of 522.8 square metres, it is endowed with many favourable geological conditions for the development. After the accomplishment of the construction for a short period of time, there appear one after another futuristic structures and facilities, including the Oriental TV Tower, Zenmao Building, Yangpu Bridge, Nanpu Bridge, Fengpu Bridge, Xupu Bridge, Songpu Bridge, the Pudong section of the Inner-Ring Highway, the Global Financial Centre of Shanghai, the Pudong International Airport, the Riverside Avenue and the Century Boulevard. Meanwhile, with the establishment of the Central Park and several development zones, including Lujiazui Finance and Trade Zone, Jinqiao Export Processing Zone, Waigaoqiao Free Trade Zone, Zhangjiang Hi-tech Zone, Huaxia Tourism Development Zone and Sunqiao Modern Agriculture Zone, the special feature of a futuristic metropolis is thus formed. And now, the Pudong New Area has doubled its effort to turn itself into a truly international city.

Situated on the eastern bank of the Huangpu River at Lujiazui in Pudong New Area, the Oriental TV Tower is Shanghai's new landmark dominating the skyline. The height of this building is second only to Toronto TV Tower in Canada and the Ostenkin TV Tower at Moscow in the Federal Russia. Covering more than 55,000

36

47.龙墙。豫园共有 5 条巨龙装饰围墙，这是其中之一。

There are totally five white curving walls topped by the undulating body of a dragon. Here is one of them.

48.豫园内景——隔水花墙

The flowery wall used to separate the stream in the Yu Garden.

49.快楼冬雪

A scene of Kuailou (Hall of Quickness) covered with snow in the winter.

50.玉玲珑与玉华堂。玉华堂前，有一块高达 3 米许的青石。青石上、下都是孔。中国古人评价石头需具备"漏、透、皱、瘦"的特点，才算石中之宝。玉玲珑全部具备了这四个条件。当年园主潘允端

得此石后，兴致勃勃地建造了一座华美的厅堂，命名玉华堂。

Yulinglong (Exquisite Jade Rock) and Yuhuatang (Hall of Jade Magnificence). This Exquisite Jade is said to have been intended as a gift for Emperor Huizong of the Song Dynasty. In this way, being treated as the relics, it has been located in front of the hall.

51.点春堂。建于清道光（1821～1850年）初年。1853 年，太平天国起义，这里曾是"上海小刀会"的指挥所。

Dianchuntang (Hall of Heralding Spring) was built in the first year of the reign of Emperor Daoguang (1821-1850) during the Qing Dynasty. During the Taiping Heavenly Kingdom period, some citizens of Shanghai, known as the Society of Little Swords, joined the peasant uprising. They used this hall as their headquarters.

square metres, it was completed in 1994.

It is the Oriental TV Tower that has dominated the cityscape of Pudong. The pinnacle of this tower has viewing areas for spectacular panoramas of the harbour, the old city areas and Riverside Avenue's new landscaped riverfront terraces along the eastern bank of the Huangpu River.

Situated on the western bank of Huangpu River in Pudong New Area, Zenmao Building stands just opposite to the Oriental TV Tower. With a prime location in the business heart of the Lujiazui Finance and Trade Zone, the Zenmao Building is quite convenient from both the Tunnel of Yan'an Rd East and the No. 2 Metro Line. Covering a total area of 290,000 square metres, the building has 88 levels and 3 being underground. Reputed as a landmark to usher in the 21st century, it ranks first in China and third in the world. The 420.5-metre-high Zenmao Building is next only to 450-metre-high Petronas Twin Towers at Kuala Lumpur in Malaysia and the Hills Building at Chicago in the United States. A perfect combination of the Oriental architecture with the modern hi-tech achievement, the Zenmao Building and the Oriental TV Tower are acclaimed as the two masterpieces in the modern history of Chinese archtecture. In the 88th level of this architectural giant there is a viewing deck and, by taking a high-speed elevator, the sightseers could get there merely in 45 seconds. Besides, along the Century Boulevard there are many other magnificent facilities, such as the wall to guard against possible flooding, riverside avenues, sightseeing terraces, musical fountains and yacht docks. As a result, the Riverside Boulevard is reputed as the New Bund of Shanghai. The first phase of the project includes a 1,500-metre-long stretch of street from Dongchang Ferry in the south to the Tongtai Wharf in the north. So, with the construction of a flyover to connect the Oriental TV Tower with the Fortune World, a brand-new scenic spot will spring up to attract more and more tourists from both home and abroad.

52

53

52.豫园内的古戏台
The ancient stage in Yu Garden is the oldest and best-preserved stage in Shanghai.

53.湖心亭的茶楼，已有 217 年的历史。
The Huxingting Teahouse was built 217 years age.

54.外国游客喜乘豫园商城中的花轿
The foreign tourists take interet in ridding a bridal sedan chair in the Yu Garden.

55.老城隍庙
The Old City God Temple.

56.豫园商城凝晖阁
Yihui Tower in the Yu Garden Bazzar.

57.九曲桥和湖心亭冬雪
The Bridge of Nine Turning and the Huxingting (Mid-lake) Teahouse in a snowy day.

58.古猗园内的唐经幢，距今已有 1130 余年历史。八角七级幢柱、尼罗经文、罗汉浮雕、卷云仰莲，造型壮丽挺秀，出于盛唐工艺，巧夺天工。

　　Located in the Guyi Garden, the Tang-dynasty stone pillar with Buddhist surtras was erected 1130 years ago. It has seven levels.

59.嘉定汇龙潭戏台天井
The carsion ceiling of the ancient stage at Huilong Pool in Jiading

60.松江醉白池，建于 1644—1661 年间。园内宋、明以来的名人碑碣、石刻，其中以"云间邦彦图"最为著名。

　　Built in the years 1644-1661, the Zuibai Pool has housed a good number of stone steles and sculptures produced during the Song and the Ming Dynasties, and the most famous of them is entitled "A Picture of Bang Yan Amidst the Clouds.,,

61.位于嘉定区的汇龙潭始建于 1588 年
Located in Jiading County, Huilong Pool was built in 1588.

62.古典园林曲水园，位于青浦县，始建于 1745 年。
Built in 1745, the Qushui Yuan (the Garden of Meandering Stream) locates in Qingpu County.

63.位于嘉定区南翔镇的古猗园，始建于 1746 年。园内不系舟，建于明代。造型奇特，舟上有楼、廊、亭、阁，参差典雅。

　　Located in Nanxiang Town, Jiading Courty, Guyi Garden was built in 1746. It is noted for having a "United Boat,, (a small pavilion in the shape of a boat, built on a stone base in one of the garden's lakes.).The garden still retains many features of the traditional Chinese garden in its pavilions, lakes, corridors, winding paths and bridges.

64.嘉定孔庙
The Confucian Temple in Jiading

65.位于松江县的兴圣教寺塔（松江方塔），建于1068年。
Built in 1068, the Square Pagoda is located at the courtyard of Xingshengjiao Temple in Songjiang.

66.位于松江县的唐代经幢，建于871年，是上海地面上最古老的文物之一。
 Erected at Songjiang in 871, the Tang-dynasty stone pillar with Buddhist sutras is one of the oldest relics wellpreserved in Shanghai

67.天恩桥，位于嘉定区南翔镇，建于明代。
 Built during the Ming Dynasty, the Tian'an Bridge is located at Nanxiang in Jiading.

68.位于嘉定区南翔镇的南翔寺砖塔（双塔），已有千余年的历史。

The Twin Pagodas at Nanxiang Town in Jiading District has a history of more than one thousand years.

69.位于松江县天马山上的护珠宝光塔，建于1079年，塔身倾斜30°而不倒。

Located on the top of Tianma Hill, the Huzhu (Pearl Protecting) Pagoda was erected in 1079. It looks just like the Piza pagoda in Italy.

70.位于松江县的西林塔建于1265～1274年间，是上海现存最高的塔。

Built during the years 1265-1274, the Xiling Pagoda stands in Songjiang County. It is the earliest well-preserved pagoda in Shanghai.

71.塔是佛教建筑。汉代随佛教传入中国。

It is a Buddhist pagoda built in the ancient time.

72.上海青浦县朱家角老街

The Ancient Street at Zhujiajiao Town in Qingpu County.

73.松江明刻照壁，明洪武三年（公元1370年）建。以一怪兽为主体，砖刻线条细致，画面生动。

Erected in 1370 during the reign of the Ming-dynasty Emperor Hongwu, the Screen Wall is decorated with a massive brick bas-relief to depict an impossing legendary beast.

74.位于青浦县朱家角镇的放生桥

The Fangsheng (Freeing Captive Creatures) Bridge, east of Zhujiajiao Town in Qingpu County, has five arches.

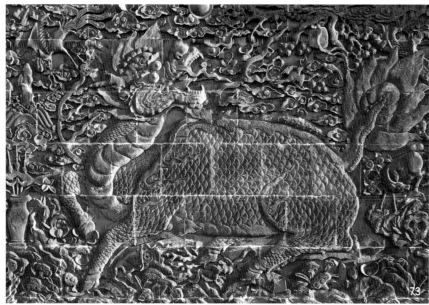

75.淀山湖大观园游览区位于上海市西南角，东临淀山湖，西靠元荡。是根据中国古典文学名著《红楼梦》的笔意，运用中国传统园艺手法建造的仿古建筑群。

Loctated in the southwestern corner of Shanghai, the Garden of Grand View Resort stands beside Diangshan Lake. The buildings and layout of the garden reproduce the garden of the same name in the classical novel *A Dream of the Red Mansions.*

76.省亲别墅

The Villa of Visiting Parents.

77.觐见礼台 —— 元妃省亲行国礼座。

The ceremonial terrace where Imperial Concubine Yuan interviewed her parents, kinsmen and kinswomen.

78.一拜天地

First of all, the bride and groom postrate themselves before the Heaven and the Earth.

79.二拜高堂

Secondly, they prostrate themselves before the groom's parents.

80.夫妻对拜

Thirdly, they prostrate themselves to each other.

81.喜入洞房

Finally, the groom accompanies the bride to enter their bridal chamber.

82.龙华寺建于唐代，后历经兴废，清光绪年间重建。是一组完整的佛寺建筑群。

Longhua Town in the southwestern suburbs is famous for its ancient temple and pagoda.

83.壮观的佛事

The magnificent atmosphere of a Buddhist ceremony held in this famous temple.

84.龙华寺中的千手观音像

The statue of Thousand-Arm Avalokietsvara in the Longhua Temple.

85.泥塑

A clay sculpture

86.龙华塔，相传为三国时建，唐末被毁，宋代重建。塔为砖木结构，七层八角形，高40余米；塔身的每层檐、廊，造型美观。

It is said that the pagoda in the Longhua Temple was built in 242 (during the time of the Wu Kingdom of the Three Kingdoms Period). It was destroyed during a war and rebuilt in 977 (during the Song Dynasty). Built of bricks and timber, it is the exquisite seven-storey octagonal Longhua Pagoda.

87~88.松江清真寺，元末创建，明代扩建，是上海地区最早的一座清真寺。礼拜堂面阔三间，结构为明代厅堂形式。

Built in the last years of Yuan Dynasty (1271-1368), the Mosque in Songjiang was renovated in the Ming Dynasty (1368-1644). It is the earliest mosque in the area of Shanghai.

89.玉佛禅寺百年庆典
A centenary ceremony held in the Jade Buddha Tomple.

90.玉佛禅寺内供奉的释迦牟尼坐像，高1.9米，系僧人慧根于清光绪初年（公元1875年）由缅甸迎来。

The jade statue of Sakyamuni (1.9m high) in the Jade Buddha Temple was brought from Myanmar by the monk Huigen around 1875 (the first year of Qing Emperor Guangxu's reign).

91.静安寺位于南京西路，始建于三国时代，原名沪渎重光寺，位于吴淞江边，宋代改今名，移至现址。

Situated on Nanjing Road West, Jing'an Temple dates back to the Three Kingdoms period. Originally located on the bank of Wusong River, it was called the Chongguang Temple. During the Song Dynasty, this temple was renamed immediately after being removed to the present site.

90

91

92.徐家汇天主教堂，建于1906年。为罗马式教堂建筑，规模宏伟，造型华丽，是上海最大的天主教堂。

Built in 1906, the Goethic-style Xujiahui Cathedral is the largest Catholic place of worship in Shanghai.

93.徐家汇天主教堂内景

An interior scene of the Xujiahui Cathedral.

94.具有俄罗斯民族风格的东正教堂

It is a well-preserved Orthodox Congregation built in Russian style.

95.建在松江佘山之颠的进教之佑圣母大殿

The Catholic church on the Sheshan Hill.

# 建筑博览

建筑是凝固的音乐，它用无声的音符，演奏出动人心弦的乐章。上海建筑，包括古代建筑、近代建筑、现代建筑，构成了一部博大精深、气势恢宏的交响乐曲。其中的近代建筑，现存300多幢风格不同的高楼大厦，享有"万国建筑博览会"的美称，著名的外滩建筑群，南京东路建筑群，南京西路建筑群，江西中路建筑群，徐汇、卢湾、静安三区的花园、别墅建筑等。

上海自1843年正式开埠即开港通商，1845年订立"土地章程"，在外滩一带划定第一块租界后，英、美、法、德、日、俄、意、西、荷、挪威等国殖民者和大批商人，从上海老城区内外的居地陆续搬进租界，在中国的土地上建立了"国中之国"。他们在租界内，大兴土木，建起银行、洋行(商行)、海关、总会、旅馆等近代建筑，成为近代上海城市的重要组成部分。20世纪20～30年代，外滩的建筑作了大量重建和翻新，使今天的外滩建筑具有英国式、希腊式、哥特式、法国式、俄国式、美国芝加哥学派式、中国式、日本式的各种特色和风格，但又和谐地统一在一起，成为上海标志性的建筑群，也成为旅游建筑景观。

上海外滩建筑群，位于上海市黄浦区，滨临黄浦江，从中山东一路的延安东路口到外白渡桥旁的上海大厦，建于1873年至1937年，是上海近百年城市发展历史和近代建筑文化的缩影。它汇集了银行、海关、洋行、总会、旅馆等高楼大厦，大部分具有欧洲古典复兴(不是一味地强调柱式结构，而是注重功能、真实与自然的结合)和折衷主义(把不同风格混用到一种建筑物中)建筑风格，现为全国重点文物保护单位。这些建筑的立面构图具有明显的古典建筑三段式划分：下段是以粗犷毛石砌筑的基座层；中段采用贯通2～3层的柱廊；上段则是檐部层，建筑顶部采取特殊的处理以作为明显标志，如汇丰银行巨大半球式的穹顶，沙逊大厦金字塔状尖顶，海关大楼的方形钟楼及中国银行四方攒坡顶等。

海关大楼是外滩建筑群的主要建筑，建于1927年，由英国设计家威尔逊设计。建筑外观具有欧洲古典和近代相糅合的折衷主义风格。大楼门楣由4根巨大的罗马花岗石圆柱支撑，以高耸的钟楼为轴线，气势非凡。最高处为哥特式(垂直、尖券、尖塔形)方型钟楼。大钟仿英国伦敦国会大厦的大钟样式制作，在英国造好后运到上海组装，是世界著名大钟之一。大钟四周均可看到走时，每隔15分钟奏响一段短曲，钟声悠扬深沉，声闻5公里。海关大楼正对面的瀑布钟，在五彩灯光映照下，水帘显现出世界主要城市的时间，与海关大钟相映成趣。

汇丰银行大楼，建于1923年，原系英商汇丰银行上海分行，是近代外商设在上海较大的银行之一。当时英国人自诩为"从苏伊士运河到远东白令海峡的一座最华贵的建筑"。该楼曾作为上海市人民政府办公大楼，现为上海浦东发展银行。大楼平面接近正方形，整座建筑除中部7层外，余皆5层。大楼为钢框架结构，半圆形的穹顶是仿古罗马万神庙之顶而建，具有显著的欧洲古典主义(采用柱式、穹顶形式)建筑特色。此楼的设计也出自英国设计家威尔逊之手，与海关大楼一起被称为"姐妹楼"，目前仍是上海的重要标志之一。

和平饭店位于南京东路口两侧，由南北两幢大楼组成，占地7000平方米，建筑面积4.8万平方米。坐南朝北的南楼建于1906年，当时称汇中饭店，是上海最早的一家饭店。其建筑立面采用红砖做腰线，白墙砖做贴面，显得庄重典雅，别具风格。坐北朝南的北楼原为英籍犹太人沙逊(以贩卖军火、鸦片起家)所建的沙逊大厦华懋饭店，1928年建，为钢筋混凝土结构，14层，高77米，1956年改今名。楼内汇集了9个国家不同风格的装饰和家具，富丽豪华。建筑外墙用花岗岩贴面，立面处理成简洁的垂直线条，是当时流行的美国芝加哥学派的设计手法(芝加哥学

97.左：1923年建成的汇丰银行大楼，室内饰以古典式藻井天花板，爱奥尼克式廊柱，为新古典主义风格建筑。
右：1927年建成的原江海北关关署。
(Left)Erected in 1923, the Hongkong and Shanghai Bank building was built in new classical style. The inside of the dome of this building has 33 pannels of mosaic pictures.
(Right) Erected in 1927, it is the Beiguan Custom House in Jianghai.

98. 1928年建成的原沙逊大厦，现为和平饭店。楼内有英、法、德、意、印、中等多国风格的建筑。
Originally known as Sassoon House, the Peace Hotel was built in 1928.It is noted for its structures being constructed in the style of many countries, including the Britain, France, Germany, Italy and India.

99.华山路上的丁香花园，为清末名臣李鸿章所建。
Located on Huashan Road, the Dingxiang Garden was built by Li Hongzhang, a high official of the Qing Dynasty.

100.上海三山会馆建于清宣统元年（公元1909年），为福建旅沪水果商人同业行会活动的场所。1927年3月，上海工人第三次武装起义时，曾做过工人纠察队沪南总部。馆址在半淞园路15号。
Built in the first year of the regin of Emperor Xuantong (1909) during the Qing Dynasty, the Sanshan Guild Hall was a place for the fruiterers coming to Shanghai from Fujian Province. During the third uprising by the Shanghai workers in March 1927, it was used as the headquarters of the south Shanghai Workers' Pickets.

99

100

派，重视功能，强调形式服从功能)。腰线和檐部带有艺术装饰派常用的纹样。顶部冠以19米高的铜绿色金字塔状的尖顶，具有19世纪末美国近代高层建筑风格。曾有"远东第一楼"的美称。

中国银行大楼，建成于1937年，是外滩建筑群中惟一由中国建筑师陆谦设计、具有中国传统特色的高层建筑。前面主楼地面上17层，地下室2层，钢架结构。后面配楼4层为混凝土结构。整幢大楼呈塔状，顶部冠以暗蓝色平缓的四方攒屋顶，檐部有斗拱作为装饰，正面两侧配以镂空格窗。此楼原设计为34层，由于沙逊是公共租界工部局董事，出面阻挠，提出不得超过沙逊大厦金字塔尖。最后改为17层，比沙逊大厦还低0.3米。楼建成后，上海建筑工人在楼顶两侧竖起了粗长的旗杆，它的高度远远超过了金字塔尖，气得沙逊"哇哇"乱叫，听说为此还生了一场大病。

南京东路建筑群，在外滩至西藏中路之间，拥有大新公司，建于1934年，现为全市最大的第一百货商店；永安公司，建于1918年，今为华联商厦；新新公司，建于1935年，今为第一食品商店；先施公司，建于1915年，现为上海时装店等。以上这4家公司当时被称为上海的四大公司，是当时上海商业繁荣的象征。南京西路建筑群，从西藏中路至静安寺，是以国际饭店高层建筑为主体的旅馆、饭店、娱乐、商业等综合建筑群。其建筑特征有古典折衷式、近代立体式、现代摩天大楼及现代商业建筑，风格多样，错落有致，统一协调，是上海城市又一处标志性建筑。江西中路建筑群，汇集了20世纪二三十年代不同形式的建筑群，有古典复兴式、哥特式、美国殖民式、近代立体式和现代国际式等。上海西区的徐汇、卢湾、静安三区，在浓密的梧桐树的掩映下，可以看到西班牙式花园洋房，法式、意大利式和英国乡村式别墅等近代建筑。比较有代表性的是：西班牙花园式建筑，位于新华路211弄；意大利式别墅，位于岳阳路中国画苑；德国式住宅建筑，位于岳阳路老干部局；法国古典主义建筑风格(崇奉柱式，突出轴线，讲求对

54

101.新浦东与城隍庙，现实与历史的写照，上下七百年，相映生辉。

Pudong New Area and the City God Temple—a portrial true to a history of seven hundred years in Shanghai.

102～104.豫园建筑顶部的屋盖、兽脊、铺瓦、排山沟滴的曲线和轮廓，上部巍然高耸，檐部如翼轻展，成为整个建筑物美丽的冠冕，体现了中国传统建筑鲜明的民族特色。

Built in traditional Chinese architectural style, theYu Garden demonstrates perfectly the sophisticated art of combining several different elements to create a world in miniature and each section is divided up by white curvring walls.

105～108.上海素有"世界建筑博览会"的美誉，风格各异的各国建筑，是城市发展的缩影，历史风云的见证。

Reputed as the "Architectural Fair of the World," Shanghai boasts a vast variety of buildings erected in multifarious style. So, it is the epitome of the long development of this world-known metropolis.

称，使用穹顶)的官邸住宅，位于汾阳路79号；仿欧洲皇宫的大理石建筑，现为上海少年宫。全楼用大理石装饰，规模宏大，富丽堂皇。1936年建成的位于陕西路的马勒住宅，为挪威式建筑，外形凹凸变化很多，屋面陡峭，主塔高大，好像童话世界里的建筑。

位于徐汇区华山路849号的丁香花园，为美国式花园别墅，著名建筑师艾赛亚·罗杰斯设计。原为清朝大官僚李鸿章(1823~1901年)的别墅。拥有3幢楼房，其中2号楼建于19世纪50年代，另二幢建于19世纪末，1号楼正面中间凸出呈梯形，为李鸿章妾丁香所居，楼前种丁香，并有香樟、棕榈。三幢别墅之南有大草坪，缭以龙墙、龙门，还有水池，上有九曲桥，中心有凤亭，八角攒尖顶，上立一凤。另建有船舫等。

桂林公园位于徐汇区漕河泾镇西桂林路1号，占地52亩(3.5万平方米)。该园原为上海青帮头子黄金荣家墓园，初建于1931年，原名黄家花园。1956年改今名。园中堆山叠石，筑有亭台楼阁，颇具古典园林风格。建国后进行了改建，调整了园林布局。园内广植桂花，有金桂、银桂、丹桂、四季桂、月月桂、刺桂等，颇具桂林特色。每逢中秋节日，桂花盛开，芳香馥郁，吸引了大批游客，盛时日达2万余人次。新建仿古建筑与原有长廊、水榭、厅堂、亭台、山石相得益彰，交映生辉。从1981年起，每年9月末，徐汇区以此园桂花盛开为主题，举办桂花节，备受中外游人青睐。

在上海近代建筑史中，石库门民居里弄住宅建筑占有一席之地。它形成于19世纪70年代，代表上海市区民居风格，是了解上海人民生活的一个窗口。石库门式里弄建筑，其单体平面式样脱胎于我国传统的三合院和四合院形式，而平面布局则吸收了欧洲联排式住宅特点。石库门住宅最有特征的是正面大门，它有一对乌漆厚实的木板门，门上装有一对铜吊环，显得庄严肃穆。门框都用粗实厚重的花岗岩和宁波红石凿成。从外立面看，除后侧厨房间有个小小的单扇后门外，整幢建筑对外再没有开口的，形成全封闭式，好比存放货物的仓库。加之以石质门框，坚固难

109.上海马戏城
The Shanghai Circus Troupe.

110.上海影城
The Shanghai Film Art Center.

111.上海海关大楼
Shanghai Custom House.

112.广电大厦
Shanghai Broadcasting and TV Building.

113.上海工业展览馆周边地区
The area around the Shanghai Industrial Exhibition.

114.上海工业展览馆
Shanghai Industrial Exhibiiion.

115.通往外滩的城市高架路
The elevated highway leading to the Bund.

116.延安路和成都路口交叉的城市高架路
    The intersection of the elevated highway between Chengdu
Road and Yan'an Road.

破，故称"石库"，门称"石库门"，那房子当然就叫"石库门住宅"了。其基本格局是，进石库门有一个露天小院，10平方米左右，上海人称作天井，是采光透气、全家户外活动的场所。正中是20平方米上下的客堂，客堂左右两侧各有约25平方米的长方形房间2间，称东西厢房。此外还有灶间、亭子间、露天晒台等。

最著名的石库门建筑就是中共一大会址，现已被列为全国重点文物保护单位。当年这里是法租界望志路106号，现在是兴业路76号。这是两栋具有上海市区典型民居风貌的砖木结构的二层石库门楼房，建于1920年，属贝勒路树德里(今黄陂南路374弄)，是一大代表李汉俊及其兄李书诚夫妇租下作为寓所的。石库门楣上有巴洛克式(外形自由，追求动态，喜好富丽的装饰和雕刻及强烈的色彩)图案装饰，红黑相间的清水墙，石库门两侧的壁柱，古朴典雅富丽，给人以庄严幽静之感。进门过天井，底层是一间18平方米的客堂，这就是1921年7月中共一大会议召开的场所。毛泽东、董必武等13名代表出席这次大会。客堂后有木梯通二楼内室。后面经过夹道到灶间，有后门通弄堂。当年法租界巡捕房密探正是从后门闯入会场的，后来代表们也是从这里转移去嘉兴南湖船上继续举行大会，并成立了中国共产党。这幢普普通通的石库门住宅，在上海近代建筑史上写下了光辉的一页。

117.中国共产党第一次全国代表大会 1921 年 7 月，就在上海兴业路 76 号（原望志路 106 号），这典型的石库门房子中召开的。

The First National Congress of the Communist Party of China was held in Shanghai in July 1921. This is the meeting site, 76 Xingye Road (106 Wangzhi Road in the old days).

118.昔日臭水沟，今日肇家浜路。

Zhaojiabang Road Today. It was a sewage ditch in the old days.

119 黄浦区和静安区交界地区

The juncture of Huangpu and Jing'an Districts.

120.浦江两岸

On either side of the Huangpu River.

## 上海新天地——"昨天、今天、明天"

上海新天地是上海历史文化风貌地都市旅游景点，它以上海独特的石库门建筑旧区为基础，改造成具有国际水平的餐饮、商业、娱乐、文化的休闲步行街。

石库门是凝固在建筑上的上海历史文化，它与豫园明清建筑群、外滩金融街、南京路百货公司建筑群等交相辉映，同为上海的都市旅游景观。

位于市中心、淮海中路南侧的上海新天地，占地3万平方米，建筑面积为6万平方米、这片石库门建筑群的外表，保留了当年的砖墙、屋瓦、石库门，仿佛时光倒流，置身于20世纪30年代。但是，每座建筑内部，则按照21世纪现代都市人的生活方式、生活节奏、情感世界，度身定做，为国际画廊、时装店、主题餐厅、咖啡酒吧……。谭永麟、成龙等百位香港明星经营的"东方魅力餐饮娱乐中心"，是明星文化结合餐饮的创意。那里是追星族经常可以与心中偶像交流的场所；台湾著名电影演员杨慧姗经营的琉璃工房主题餐厅，将使游客置身于七彩水晶宫中用餐；法国餐厅的巴黎歌舞表演和地下酒窖餐室令人神往；日本音乐餐厅，夜夜摇滚乐绕梁不绝；巴西烤肉餐厅，带来了南美风情表演……。

那里的时尚精品店紧追国际流行色，不逊半步，中华文化商场出售的是艺人、工匠们独创的居家用品和旅游纪念品，完全是地道的中国味。露天广场上丰富多彩的文化表演，让游客有许多的参与，石库门博物馆通过对一幢楼的重新布置、家具摆设，原汁原味地再现20世纪初上海一家人的生活形态，让游客有怀旧寻根的情绪，以了解上海的历史文化。博物馆也通过图片、录像，讲解上海新天地从石库门建筑旧区到时尚休闲步行街的演变。

121.上海石库门民居
One of the stone-arched-gate residences in Shanghai.

122.新天地广场步行街街景
A view of the pedestrian street on the Xintiandi Square.

123.杨浦区已有近 80 多年历史的里弄
The lanes in Yangpu District were built more than eighty years ago.

124.星巴克咖啡屋的石库门
The stone-arched gate of Starbucks Coffee.

125.石库门门头
The front door of a stone-arched-gate residence.

126.石库门楼花
The flowery decoration on a stone-arched-gate residence.

新天地的石库门里弄，处处体现了21世纪的舒适和方便。自动电梯、中央空调、宽带互联网一应俱全。消费者上网可以迅速查询商店的商品价格和餐厅、酒吧的菜单，以及电影院上演的电影，并且可以预订座位，还可以直接网上浏览，观赏新天地露天广场及餐馆内的文艺表演。走进新天地，更多的时尚和新潮，让人看不完也看不够；更多的参与投入，让人开心一天玩不够。这里是中外游客领略上海历史文化和现代生活形态的最佳去处。

上海新天地亦古亦今、亦西亦中的建筑风格和经营特色，让人耳目一新。从脚手架尚未拆落的那一刻起，各路明星、艺术家、企业家、银行家、驻沪外交官纷至沓来，流连忘返。国际模特儿大赛、时装表演、日本太鼓座表演、著名影星的电影新闻发布会等时尚文活动，纷纷选择在上海新天地登场亮相。这个崭新的国际大都市的时尚休闲之地，为昨天的石库门，营造了更加辉煌璀璨的明天。

127.年代久远的石库门老宅
A well-preserved old stone-arched-gate residence in Shanghai.

128.石库门老住宅区
The stone-arched-gate residence lane

129.保持石库门建筑特色、整旧如旧、精装修的餐厅内景
The elegant interior of a restaurant on the Xintiandi Square.

130.石库门内部已十分现代了
All of the interiors in this stone-arched-gate residence complex are quite modern and fashionable.

131.地中海风味的璐娜餐厅
Luna Restaurant is designed and decorated with the Mediterranean flavour.

132.新天地的石库门弄堂
The lane of stone-arched-gate residences where Xintiandi (Brand-New Field) is located.

## Shanghai Xintiandi (Brand-New Field) — Where Yesterday & Tomorrow Meet Today

Shanghai Brand-New Field, a newly-emerged tourist attraction in the downtown area, features how the city's unique "Shikumen" (the stone-arched-gate residence) in a maze of narrow alleys has been converted into one of the most fashionable F&B, retail, entertainment and cultural facilities in Shanghai.

Built in the late 19th and early 20th centuries, Shikumen (stone-arched-gate residence) is a special form of residence in Shanghai. Just like the Ming-and-Qing-dynasty classical structures in the Yu Garden, the bank buildings on the Bund and the department stores along the Nanjing Road, Shikumen residence is also a symbol of Shanghai's history and tourism resources.

Located south of Huaihai Road Middle, the Brand-New Field is a fashionable mall accommodated with the dining and recreation facilities. It has a land area of 30,000 square meters and a gross floor space of 60,000 square meters within a renovated complex of stone-arched-gate residence. All of the structures have retained their original exterior: brick walls, tiled roofs and stone-framed black wooden gates, making visitors feel as if they were back to the 1920s Shanghai. In reality, however, each structure in this complex is fully equipped to meet the needs of the new century.

A wide variety of institutions, such as the international art galleries, fashion boutiques, restaurants, cafes and bars, are located in the Brand-New Field. No doubt, the restaurant entitled "Oriental Charm", a dining and entertainment center invested by 100 Hong Kong show-biz celebrities including Jackie Chan and Alan Tam, has become a haunt for the locals. Yang Huishan, a wellknown Taiwan film actress, has opened a restaurant modeled after her Art Glass Studio. The La Maison features Parisian-style cabaret show and cellar-inspired dining rooms; the Xintiandi ARK vibrates every night with rock "n" roll; while Latina spices up its Brazilian grills with flamboyant Latin dances.

In the Brand-New Field, consumers can find any of the latest fashions in the world as well as the best commodities and souvenirs produced by the excellent Chinese craftsmen. On the central square outside the entrance there is a stage to offer various artistic performances. Meanwhile, the Museum of the Stone-Arched-Gate Residences displays the model of a typical Shikumen housedhold with original furniture and daily articles. It shows at the same time how the Brand-New Field has become a stylish mall from a timeworn neighborhood through both pictures and videos.

Modern amenities are avaliable everywhere in this plaza, such as automatic escalators, central air-conditioning and broadband Internet connections. Consumers can get online information about any shops and restaurants there, including the prices, menus and cinema programmmes. They can also make reservations online. Tourists can watch outdoor performances on the central square or enjoy the cabaret shows in a restaurant. There is just too much to enjoy in a day in the Brand-New Field. The whole area is bound to become an icon on the city tourist map and a favorite hangout for both the locals and expatriates.

The mix of old and new, the Chinese and the Western architecture, and the unique characteristics of all shops and recreational facilities have made the Brand-New Field a hot property. Long before the scaffolding had been completely removed, celebrities, entrepreneurs, bankers and foreign diplomats began to come and visit one after another. Ever since its establishment, the Brand-New Field has hosted a number of international fashion shows, modeling contests, film release, press conferences and other highly recommended events.

133.新天地石库门博物馆外墙
A wall of the Stone-Arched-Gate Residence Museum on the Xintiandi Square.

134.老式公寓房
An apartment built in the old style.

135.虹桥经济技术开发区
Hongqiao Economic and Technological Development Zone.

136.淮海中路以南地区的巨大变化
A great change in the area south of Huaihai Road Middle.

## The Architectural Fair

Architecture is a kind of condensed music and its moving melody is performed by a series of soundless notes. So does the architecture in Shanghai: it is the community of structures including the ancient, modern and contemporary products, that have constituted a grand and profound symphony. Erected in different style over the previous hundred years, more than 300 buildings built in different style (including those on the Bund, the Nanjing Road East, the Nanjing Road West, and the Jiangxi Road Middle), as well as the gardens and villas in the Xuhui, Luwan and Jing'an districts were reputed as the "International Fair of Architecture".

Shortly after the formal operation as an open trade port in 1843, the Land Chapter was signed in 1845. So, with the establishment of the first piece of enclave, the colonists from many foreign countries (including the Britain, USA, French, Germany, Japan, Russia, Italy, Spanish, Netherlands and Norway) and the foreign traders resided originally in the Old Town swarmed in to establish their settlements. As a consequence, they went in for large-scale construction. Before long, there appeared banks, companies, customs, clubs and hotels and, what's more, all of structures had become later on the important part of the consmopolitan aspect of Shanghai in its heyday. During the Twenties and Thirties of the last century, with the accomplishment of a grand renovation and reconstruction, there emerged a good number of high-rises in different style (such as the British, the Greek, the Goethic, the French, Russian, Chinese, Japanese and the Chicago style of the United States). Getting together in perfect harmony dispite of being different in style, they had become the landmark architectural complex in Shanghai. Lying along west bank of Huangpu River, the architectural complex on the Bund is an epitome of the development of Shanghai over the previous ninety-odd years from 1873 to 1937. Built either in European classical Renanssance style or in the

137.国家建设部在上海的试点住宅小区——万里小区
    The Wanli Residential Area—a place where an experiment is made by the Ministry of Construction

138.乞都苑住宅小区
Mingduyuan Residential Area.

139.苏州河及两岸环境，得以改善。
    The newly-emerged green space on the either side of the Suzhou Creek.

140.延安中路绿地——城市"绿肺"工程
 A green space on Yan'an Road Middle.

eclectist style, they have all become the relics under the state protection. Having analysed the plane composition of these structures, we will soon come to the conclusion that the architects had applied the same division method: the base was laid out by stones in the lower part, the 2-3 storey-high pillars were applied in the middle part while the top was usually placed as a symbol. For instance, the Hong Kong and Shanghai Bank bulding – an enormous ball-shaped top; the Sassoon House – a 19-metre green pyramidal roof; the Custom House – a four-sided clock tower; the Shanghai branch of the Bank of China – a roof with four rising edges and decorative gutters at the eaves.

Erected in the middle of the Bund in 1927 and designed by Mr. Wilson (a British architect), the Custom House was.supporting by four Roman granites in its front. According to the expert, the structure is an outcome of Western architectural influence with few classical decorations. The Westminister on the four-sided clock tower atop ring every quarter hour, aidding to the romance and beauty of the waterfront. Built in 1923, the Hong Kong and Shanghai Bank bilding is characerized by three granite arches at the front gate and an enormous ball-shaped top. At that time, this building was once boasted as "the finest and most impossing anywhere between the Suez Canal and the Bering Strait." Used as the location of the Municipal government after the founding of PRC in 1949, it is now housed by the Development Bank of Pudong, Shanghai. Known as "the sister buildings" together with the Custom House, they are regarded as one of Shanghai's landmarks even at the present time.

Constituted of two buildings, the Peace Hotel (called the Cathay and Palace Hotels before 1949), stands on either side of the eastern end of Nanjing Road East. The southern building was built in 1906 and it was the earliest hotel in Shanghai. Erected in 1928, the northern building, widely known as the Sassoon House, is a special attraction of the Bund for its 19-metre green pyramidal roof. It is reputed as the "First Building in the Far East."

世 纪 花 钟

FLOWER CLOCK

花钟直径为12米, 指针为航天铝镁合金复合材料, GPS
卫星校时, 日误差±0.03秒 2000年1月1日零点报时

141.大型城市不锈钢雕塑——世纪之光
The Centenary Light — a large sculplture made of stainless steel.

142.世纪公园中的世纪花钟
The flower clock at the Century Park.

143.路边雕塑
A roadside sculpture.

144.普希金雕像
　　The statue of Aleksander Sergeevich Pushkin, a great Russian poet, on Fenyang Road.

145.城市雕塑——奋进
"Dash ahead!„( one of the sculptures in Shanghai)

146.城市雕塑——上海欢迎您
"You Are Welcome to Shanghai!„( one of the sculptures in Shanghai)

Built in 1937, the Shanghai branch of the Bank of China is designed by Lu Qian, a Chinese architect. It is the only building along the Bund that glitters with Chinese traditional flavour. Its roof has four rising edges and decorative gutters at the eaves. Besides, its window glass patterns are also typical Chinese. The main structure of this building has 17 levels and 2 being underground. Originally, the main structure was planned to erect 34 storeys. Hearing this, Sir Sassoon, a member of the Public Council, soon raised an opposition, demanding that the height of his neighbouring structure shouldn't surpass that of his House. As a consequence, the new one was reduced to an edifice with 17 storeys, 0.3 metre low than the old one. However, with the erecting of a long and thick flagpole by some building workers on the top of the new imposing edifice, the height of the latter had far surpassed that of the former. This made Sir Sassoon very angry and, what's more, he soon fell seriously ill on account of this setback.

Spread along the either side of Nanjing Road East stretching from the Bund to Xizang Road Middle, there stands another well-known complex of imposing high-rises in Shanghai. The Sun (now the No. 1 Department Store) was built in 1934; the Wing On (now the Hualian Department Store) was erected in 1918; the Sun Sun (now the No. 1 Food Store) was completed in 1935; the Sincere (now the Shanghai Fashion Dress Store) was constructed in 1915. Collectively known as "the Four Grand Companies of Shanghai", they are the symbol of the city's prosperous commerce at that time. Lined up along the Nanjing Road West from Xizang Road Middle to the Jing'an Temple, stands the third well-known architectural complex in Shanghai. With the Park Hotel as its centre, they are magnificent hotels, restaurants, entertainment grounds and shops. Built in multifarious style, they are quite harmonious though in picturesque disorder. Situated along the Jiangxi Road Middle, the high-rises were all built during the Twenties and Thirties.

147.南京路步行街世纪广场夜色
　　The night view of the Century Square at the pedestrian street on Nanjing Road

148.众多的街头公园，发挥着平衡市区生态环境的功能。
　　Shanghai boasts a good number of street parks. They have played an important role in improving the ecological condition of this city.

149.市区中心绿地
The major green space in the centre of Shanghai.

150.上海植物园
The Shanghai Botanical Garden

71

Their architectural style includes the classical Renassance, gothic, American colonial and modern three-dimensional style. Besides, there are numerous mansions in the French, Spanish and English style. Most of them have become the architectural relics. For example, the marble building built in the shape of an Europan palace (now, it is used as the Shanghai Young Pioneers' Palace) and Mr Moller's residence in Norway style on Shaanxi Road. Built in 1936, the Moller's House looks just like a building appeared time and again in the world of fairy tales.

Located at 849 Huashan Road in Xuhui District, Dingxiang Garden is a colonial era villa designed by an American architect by the name of E. Rogers. Originally, it was Li Hongzhang (1823-1901), a high official during the last period of the Qing Dynasty, who built this residence for his concubine Ding Xiang. So, apart from being accommodated with a series of facilities in traditional Chinese style (such as courtyard, garden, pool, screen, stone boat and pavilion), lilac grows everywhere in this private mansion.

Located at No. 1 Guilin Road West in the southwestern suburbs, the Guilin Park was erected on the basis of the Huang Family Garden built in the Suzhou style in 1933 by Huang Jinrong (one of the notorious gangsters in Shanghai. With the change of its name, the park had undergone a series of renovation. So, it is now a very pleasant place particularly in early autumn when the fragrant *guihua* (osmanthus) flowers are in bloom. Ever since 1981, the Osmanthus Flower Festival is held at the end of September every year.

In Shanghai's modern history of architecture, *shikumen* (the residence for the common inhabitants) has occupied an important position. Formed during the seventies of the 19th century, the building had reflected the characteristic spirit of the Shanghaineses, so it is the window through which you may have a good understanding of their customs and life. Having imitated the layout of *siheyuan* (quadrangle), the dwelling is built in the for-

151.浦东滨江大道的绿化、美化环境。
The green space on the Riverside Avenue in the Pudong New Area.

152.衡山路法国梧桐林荫大道
The Hengshan Road is lined with French parasol trees.

153.城市轻轨铁路
The newly-opened light rail.

73

mat of two-storey houses with a little court-yard in the centre of the fore part. The most chararacteristic feature is its front gate with a pair of wooden leaves, which, painted usually in black colour and decorated with brass rings on either side, is constructed with four stone doorframes. So, the front door looks quite magnificent. Despite of bcing small in scale, the building is accommodated with many necessary facilities, including bed rooms, kitchen, guest room, courtyard as well as the flat roof for drying clothes. Since the whole building looks just like a warehouse, it was known as "*shikumen*" (stone warehouse).

The most famous "shikumen" is the site of the First National Congress of the Communist Party of China. Located at 76 Xingye Road (106 Wangzhi Road in the old days), a small street near Fuxing Park, it is a beautifully restored grey brick house. The Congress was held in July 1921, at which the birth of the Communist Party of China was declared. The opening meetng took place at 127 Taichang Road, but it was here, at the home of one of the founding members, that the 12 delegates, among them Mao Zedong, held the bulk of their discussions. The meeting was interrupted by a stranger believed to be a spy from the French police. The delegates immediately stopped the meeting and withdrew to Jiaxing County, 113 kilometres (70 miles) south of Shanghai in Zhejiang Province, where they resumed their deliberations on a pleasure boat on Nanhu Lake.This ordinary dwelling house has, therefore, opened a glorious page in the history of Chinese architecture.

154.杨浦大桥，跨度602米，为世界第一叠合梁斜拉桥。
The Yangpu Bridge.

155.南浦大桥，全长8346米，是上海市区第一座跨越黄浦江的双塔双索斜拉桥。
The Nanpu Bridge.

156.徐家汇城市内环线高架路
The inner ring elevated expressway at Xujiahui.

157.人民广场周围地区发展规划的沙盘模型
The model of the future urban construction around the People's Square.

158.地铁一号线、二号线和轻轨明珠三号线的开通，使上海的城市公共交通更为便捷畅通。
The accomplishment of the Metro No.1 Line, No.2 Line and the Light Rail Pearl Line No.3 have made the communication in Shanghai more easy and quick..

159.漕溪路立交桥
A flyover at Caoxi Road.

# 海派风情

上海，背靠中国大陆的锦绣山河，紧依横贯九域的万里长江，面对浩瀚无垠的太平洋，是一个典型的海洋性城市，形成了襟江带海、吞吐万汇的地理优势，开阔了上海人的视野，哺育了上海人的开放品格。上海人经历了悠远多彩的古代历史，继承了中国古老的传统文化，受到了潜移默化的影响。近百年的中国近代史把上海推向了中西文化交融碰撞的前沿阵地，西方文明的激流挟带着污泥浊水席卷而来，在大上海这块风水宝地上撞合、喧哗，卷起狂涛巨澜。上海人在这奔腾激流的洗礼中，形成了不拘陈规、敢于创新、兼收并蓄、发扬光大、走向世界、开辟未来的海派风格。1993年成立浦东新区，扩大开放，上海进入了新的历史发展时期。上海人的海派风格更发挥得淋漓尽致，尽善尽美。上海人不仅有走向世界的勇气，还有纵横世界的气概。上海人的海派风格应该是更开放、更强健、更热烈、更辉煌。上海市近几年发生的日新月异、突飞猛进的辉煌巨变，正是上海人海派风格的集中体现。

海派风格起源于明代著名科学家徐光启。徐光启(1562～1633年)，字子先，号玄扈，上海徐家汇人。明万历进士，崇祯进官至礼部尚书，文渊阁大学士。曾从意大利传教士利马窦学习天文、历法、数学、测量、水利等西方科技知识，曾翻译《勾股义》、《几何原本》、《测量法义》、《泰西水法》等，成为"西学东渐"的开端，是我国研究和介绍西方科学的先驱，为中西文化交流的杰出代表。徐光启开通、好学、随和、机灵，既继承传统文化，著《农政全书》，对近代科学作出了突出贡献；又把心灵的门户向着世界文明洞开，兼收并蓄，发扬光大，为海派风格的形成奠定了坚实的基础。他的故居在今南市区乔家路，仅存一进，俗称"九间楼"。生前在上海城西南

160

161

76

160.热爱运动的上海人
Most of the Shanghai residents are sport fans.

161.全民健身运动蓬勃开展
The drive to improve health is quite popular in this city.

162.三年大变样　看了喜洋洋
　　Encouraged by the great change in three years, the people smile from ear to ear.

163.祖国在我心中
The Motherland Is Always in Our Hearts.

郊法华泾、肇家浜汇合处，建农庄别业，从事农业科学实验和著书立说，后子孙居此，遂称徐家汇。其墓在徐汇区南丹路光启公园内。墓前有徐光启的石雕半身像。墓冢呈椭圆形，由花岗石围成，上覆素土，披有绿草。东侧为碑廊，有徐光启画像、手迹和传记等石刻12块，为全国重点文物保护单位。在人民广场中心有"科技先辈"（即徐光启）的浮雕。在漕溪北路建国宾馆对面有徐光启塑像。

海派文化是中国形态的近代城市市民文化，起源于上海城市，是海派风格在文化领域中的集中体现。1840年鸦片战争后，形形色色的西方文化与中国的传统文化冲突融合，形成了与京派文化有所区别的海派文化。海派文化首先发端于"海上画派"。1843年上海开埠通商后，海道畅通，人文荟萃，各地书画人士挟艺流寓沪上者日众，上海渐成绘画活动中心。时人对寓居上海的画师画匠名之为"海上画派"，代表人物有赵之谦、任颐（伯年）、吴昌硕、黄宾虹等。这些画家由于较早受到新思想的冲击，不愿墨守成法的陈陈相袭。他们上承唐宋优良绘画传统，吸取明清诸家之长，又受清代金石学影响，破格创新，个性鲜明，画风趋向笔墨清新、浑厚豪放的气质，表现出一种坚韧顽强、蓬勃向上的精神。他们熔中西文化于一炉，富于生活气息和时代感，为海派文化注入了新鲜的血液，使海派文化充满勃勃生机。海派文化的突出特点是兼收并蓄，五彩缤纷；不拘陈规，勇于创新；中西交融，雅俗共赏。海派文化在中国近代文化史上占有重要地位，对各地有很强的辐射力和影响力。在上海改革开放的大潮中，海派文化必将发扬光大，充满无限的魅力。

上海是中国历史文化名城，其近代历史与文化尤为丰富多彩。1291年建城以来，特别是1843年上海开埠以后的百余年，许多重大历史事件和重要历史人物在上海留下了大量的史迹，成为近代中国的缩影。上海共有13处全国重点文物保护单位、64处上海市重点文物保护单位，具有很大的历史与文化价值。这些文物保护单位，特别是近代的文化遗迹，大多成为名扬中外

164.上海是我国商品花卉生产和销售的主要基地之一
　　Shanghai is one of the major commercial flower and plant bases of both production and sale in China.

165～166.上海姑娘
The Shanghai young girls.

167.孪生姐妹上学堂
The twin sisters go to school hand in hand.

168.舞蹈班的小朋友
The young learners at a dancing class.

169.盲人的心愿——摸一摸世纪之桥
　　To have a touch of the Century Bridge—A common wish of the blindmen.

170.社会福利院的百岁老人幸福地安度晚年
The centenarians lead a happy life in their old folk home.

171.不平凡的五岁生日——癌症患者庆新生
A birthday celebration is held for a five-year-old cancer patient.

167

168

169

70

171

的纪念地、参观点和景观线，如小刀会起义指挥部、豫园点春堂、民主革命先行者孙中山故居、国际政治活动家宋庆龄故居和宋庆龄陵园、中国共产党第一次全国代表大会会址、中国文化巨匠鲁迅故居和鲁迅墓、上海工人第三次武装起义指挥部三山会馆和中国共产党代表团驻沪办事处周公馆以及中国社会主义青年团中央机关旧址等。

上海是中国新文化运动的发祥地，其杰出代表当属中国文学家、思想家和革命家鲁迅先生（1881—1936年）。鲁迅，原名周树人，浙江绍兴人，1918年首次用笔名"鲁迅"发表第一篇白话小说《狂人日记》，大胆揭露吃人的封建礼教，奠定了新文学运动的基石。五四运动前后，参加《新青年》杂志工作，猛烈抨击封建文化与封建道德，成为新文化运动的伟大旗手。20世纪20年代，陆续出版了《呐喊》等许多专集，表现出爱国主义和彻底革命民主主义的思想特色。中篇小说《阿Q正传》是中国现代文学史上的杰作。1927年10月到达上海。1930年起先后参加了中国左翼作家联盟等革命组织，积极参加革命文艺运动，创作了许多杂文，表现出卓越的政治远见和坚韧的战斗精神，对中国革命文化事业作出了巨大的贡献。1936年病逝于上海，安息在鲁迅公园的鲁迅墓中。鲁迅永远活在人们的心中。

上海在相当长的时期内成为"群贤毕至、风云际会"的文化舞台。文学家郭沫若、郁达夫、茅盾、巴金；教育家蔡元培、陶行知；书画家吴昌硕、徐悲鸿、刘海粟；出版家张元济；新闻工作者邹韬奋；音乐家聂耳、冼星海；表演艺术家赵丹；京剧大师周信芳等一代名流的传世佳作，都曾在这里孕育问世，形成了群星灿烂的文化艺术景观。

上海的娱乐生活丰富多彩，引人入胜。主要以文艺活动为主，兼顾咖啡馆、茶艺馆、酒吧、卡拉OK、迪斯科、趣味特色吧、保龄球馆、健身场馆、网球场、高尔夫俱乐部等娱乐、休闲、健身活动。上海拥有许多海内外著名的演出团体，如上海交响乐团、上海芭蕾舞团、上海昆剧团、上海京剧团、上海杂技团、上海越剧团、上海舞剧团与和平饭店老年爵士乐队等。演出的节

173

80

172.上海复旦大学博士生毕业合影

The doctoral candidates pose for a collective photo in memory of their graduation from the Fudan University in Shanghai.

173.全市学龄前儿童入学率达到99.9%

The enrollment rate of the preschool children has reached 99.9% in Shanghai.

174.上海老年大学美术班

The fine arts class at an oldman university in Shanghai.

175 演出中的中学生交响乐队

The performance is staged by one of the Shanghai's middle-school student orchestras

176.上海金山农民画

The paintings accomplished by the Jinshan peasants in Shanghai.

177.广场音乐会
The concert held on a square in the Bund.

178.国际音乐会
An international concert.

目有交响乐、芭蕾舞、民族舞、民乐、杂技、马戏、魔术、歌剧、戏剧(沪剧、昆剧、京剧、越剧、话剧、淮剧、滑稽剧等)和曲艺(独脚戏、评弹、上海说唱等)。此外，上海还有众多的时装表演队，通俗歌手、伴奏乐队等活跃在餐厅、舞厅、歌厅和酒吧。

179. 上海是一本巨大的爱情诗集，每时每刻都在产生新的诗句。

Shanghai is one of the favourite places for the couples of newly-weds to spend their honeymoon holidays.

180. 旧式婚礼

A traditional wedding ceremony.

181. 和平饭店老年爵士乐队闻名遐迩。乐曲的韵味、绅士的风度、演出的氛围，仿佛使人置身于三四十年代。

Composed of musicians with more than fifty years' experience, the Old Musicians' Jazz Band at the Peace Hotel is wellknown both at home and abroad.

## The Culture of Shanghai School

Situated at the middle of China's long coast-line, Shanghai is endowed with a unique geographical position with Yangtze River behind it. So, ever since its being established as a port during the Yuan Dynasty, it has become the best place for attracting and distributing commodities. In such a case, the circumstance of the open port has brought about the open spirit to the locals. Later on, with the exchange of the trade and culture between China and the Western countries, it was the Shanghainese who had once again to face and experience such a great conflict. In this way, there appeared an extraordinary culture peculiar to Shanghai: the Shanghainese had to give up old habits and break new ground on the basis of absorbing all goodness coming from the West and promoting all fine elements handed down from their ancestors. In this respect, the tremendous success of reform and reconstruction achieved in this city over the previous years is none other than the embodiment of the above-mentioned Shanghai spirit.

The term "Shanghai school" is originated from the activities of Xu Guangqi. Born of a poor family on the outskirts of Shanghai, Xu Guangqi (1562-1633) was a famous scientist of the Ming Dynasty (1368-1644). By the time when he was young, Catholic priests from the West began to preach their faith in China, bringing with them at the same time Western achievements in natural science. The young man was greatly impressed by the new knowledge. Just then, he met by chance Matteo Ricci (1552-1610), the well-known Italian priest in China. With the latter's help, Xu Guangqi learned a lot about foreign language and Western knowledge about mathematics, astronomy and calendar. Convinced that these subjects were useful , he made up his mind to pursue them in earnest, starting meanwhile to translate a couple of Western scientific treatises into Chinese, such as *Trigonometry, Geometry* and *Water Conservancy*. Soon after receiving the title of *jinshi* during the reign of Emperor Wangli in the Ming Dynasty, he was made a court official responsible for political and military affairs. In his later years, he returned to his native country, where he bought a few pieces of land and started a farming estate. He kept on his scientific pursuits through experiments. Finally, on the basis of summing up the experience of his predecessors and absorbing the scientific achievements in the West, he accomplished his gigantic monograph entitled "The Complete Book on Agricultural Pursuit" (Nong Zhen Quan Shu, 1639). It is a colosal academic work describing the great achievements in agricultural science of ancient China. Since all of his children had kept on living in his old home, the place was therefore named "Xujiahui" (the gathering of Xu family members). In order to commemorate his striking deeds, a park was set up in his honour on Nandan Road. Built with granite, his oval-shaped grave is covered with pure mud and green grass. To the east side of the grave, there stands a pavilion of stone tablets, in which a stone staue of Xu Guangqi, his manuscrits and a biography on his life and twelve pieces of steles are housed. Owing to having housed a series of precious relics, the pavilion was approved as a site under the state protection. Besides, in order to commemorate this famous scientist, a relief sculpture with inscription "The Predecessor in Science" is erected on the People's Square and a statue of Xu Guangqi is erected at a place opposite to Jianguo Hotel on Caoxi Road North.

*Haipai* (Shanghai-school) culture is one of the extraordinary regional culture peculiar to the inhabitants of modern cities in China. Originated from Shanghai, it is the concentrated reflection of the Shanghai spirit in the field of culture. With the conflic and the mixture of various Western culture and the traditional Chinese culture, the Shanghai-school culture, which differs greatly from the Beijing-school culture, was formed eventually after the First Opium War in 1840. As a matter of fact, the Shanghai-style culture was originated from the painting circles in Shanghai. Ever since the founding of the Shanghai port in 1843, Shanghai was soon turned into a place with rich social and cultural resources in addition to convenient transportation. As a consequence, the painters in other regions began to move to Shanghai one after another, including the famous painters Zhao Zhiqian

182

183

上海民间收藏的规模可谓全国之最
The Shanghai's folk collection of art is reputed as the "largest in size in China".

182.算盘收藏
A collection of abscuses.

183.古玩市场
The antiques and curios market.

184~195.京剧脸谱收藏
A collection of Peking opera theatrical masks.

196.钟表收藏
A collection of old watches and clocks.

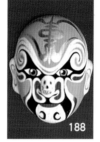

185　186　187　188

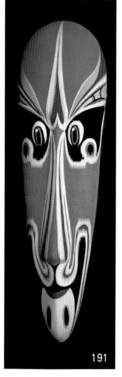

189　190　191　192　193　194　195

(1829-1884), Ren Bonian (1840-1896), Wu Changshou (1844-1927) and Huang Binghong (1865-1955). On account of their having suffered from the attack by some new idea in the process of confrontation between the Western and the Chinese culture, thus refusing to stick to the old rules in terms of the painting method. Then, on account of the fact that, while carrying on the fine tradition of the art of traditional Chinese painting during the Tang and the Song Dynasties, absorbing the strong points from the painting masters of the Ming and Qing Dynasties and, finally, being influenced by the achievements of the epigraphy during the Qing Dynasty, they began to break ground and strive to demonstrate their personnal character in their own works. As a result, all of their products are full of fresh atmosphere and high spirits. The most outstanding feature of the Shanghai-school culture is its having inherited all of the good qualities and taken in everything useful for the development of Chinese culture. In short, the *haipai* culture has occupied an important position in the modern history of Chinese culture. Meanwhile, it will play a more active role in the effort to push forward the drive of both reform and opening-up in Shanghai.

As one of the well-known historical and cultural cities in China, Shanghai is noted especially for its rich in having witnessed a couple of significant events happened in the modern and contemporary history of China. Since its establishment in 1291, and especially after becoming one of the six open ports in 1843, many important historical events were occured in Shanghai and many famous historical figures had left behind their footprints in this city. In such a case, Shanghai is none other than the epitome of modern history of China. There are 13 sites of historical interest under the state protection and 64 places under the municipal protection. Endowed with great historical and cultural significance, all of these institutions, especially the relics formed in the passage of contemporary history, have almost become either the world-known memoriable place, or the scenic spots frequented by the tourists from both home and abroad. For example, the Headquarters of the Uprising Peasants known as the Society of

197.周恩来故居
The Former Residence of Zhou Enlai (1898-1976).

198.明代科学家——徐光启塑像
The statue of Xu Guangqi(1562-1633), a well-known Ming-dynasty scientist.

199.田汉塑像
The statue of Tian Han, a well-known dramatist.

200.淮海中路 1848 号，宋庆龄故居。
The Former Residence of Madame Soong Ching-ling is located at No. 1848, Huaihai Road Middle.

201.宋庆龄塑像
The statue of Madame Soong Ching-ling.

202.香山路 7 号，孙中山故居。
The Former Residence of Dr Sun Yat-sen is located at No. 7, Xiangshan Road.

203.孙中山故居内景
Inside Dr Sun Yat-sen's Former Residence.

Little Sword, the Hall of Heralding Spring in the Yu Garden, the Former Residence of Dr Sun Yat-sen (the father of the Republic of China), the Former Residence and Mausoleum of Madam Song Ching-ling, the site of the First Congress of CPC, the Former Residence and Mausoleum of Lu Xun (the great writer of modern China), the Headquarters of the Third Uprising of Shanghai Workers at the Sanshan Guild Hall, the Former Residence of Zhou Enlai (i.e, Shanghai Office for the Delegation of the CPC in 1946) and the former location of the central organ of the Chinese Youth League of Socialism.

Shanghai is the birthplace of New Cultural Movement in China and the outstanding representative is, no doubt, Lu Xun, the well-known writer, thinker and revolutionary of modern China. Originally named Zhou Shuren, Lu Xun (1881-1936) was born in Shaoxing, Zhejiang Province. In May 1916, he published his first vernacular story "A Madman's Diary" in the magazine *New Youth*, adopting the penname Lu Xun for the first time. Having exposed boldly the cannibalistic feudal ethics, it had laid a ground stone for the development of new literary movement. Before and after the May Fourth Movement, he joined the publication of the magazine *New Youth*, giving a firm attack on both the feudal culture and feudal ethics, thus becoming the great banner of the new cultural movement. During the Twenties, he turned out a series of new poroducts, including *Call to Arms*, which were endowed with the characteristics of patriotism and revolutionary democratism. As for his novellette, *The True Story of Ah Q*, it is universally acclaimed as the masterpiece in the history of modern Chinese literature. In October 1927, he arrived at Shanghai. Ever since 1930, apart from having joined successfully the revolutionary organizations, such as the League of Chinese Left-Wing Writers, he took an active part in all the revolutionary activities and produced a good number of essays. Full of the demonstration of his excellent political foresight and formidable fighting spirit, rendering therefore a great contribution to the revolutionary cultural undertaking of China. On October 19, 1936, he died of tuberculousis in Shanghai and

204.中华人民共和国第一任上海市长
　　——陈毅铜像，屹立在黄浦江边。
　　The statue of Chen Yi, the first mayor of Shanghai.

205.坐落在鲁迅公园内的鲁迅塑像
　　The statue of Lu Xun, a world-known Chinese modern writer, is located at the Lu Xun Park in Shanghai.

206.鲁迅故居内景
Inside Former Residence of Lu Xun.

207.百岁老人绘丹青
　　——国画大师朱屺瞻
Zhu Qizhan , a noted centenarian painter.

208.著名音乐指挥家——陈燮阳
　　Chen Xieyang, a well-known musical conductor.

209.作家——巴金
Ba Jin(1904-), a famous novelist.

210.京剧表演艺术家——尚长荣
　　Shang Changrong, a well-known Peking opera actor.

his remains were buried in the tomb at the Lu Xun Park in the western part of Shanghai. However, his remarkable spirit has lived forever in the heart of the Chinese people. For a long period of time, Shanghai had been functioned as the cultural stage, on which emerged one after another the renowned celebrities, including Guo Moruo (1829-1978, a famous poet, dramatist and archaeologist), Yu Dafu (1896-1945, a well-known novelist), Mao Dun (1896-1981, a famous novelist), Ba Jin (1904 - , a famous novelist), Cai Yuanpei (1868-1940, a famous educator), Tao Xingzhi (1891-1946, a well-known educator), Wu Changshou (1844-1927, a famous painter), Xu Beihong (1895-1953, a famous painter), Liu Haisu (a well-known painter), Zhang Yuanji (1867-1949, a famous publisher), Zhou Taofen (1895-1944, a well-known journalist), Nie Er (1912-1935, a famous musician), Xian Xinghai (1905-1945, a famous musician), Zhao Dan (1915-1986, a famous film star) and Zhou Xingfang (1895-1975, a famous Peking opera actor). Having cultivated themselves and gained fame in Shanghai, all of these celebrities have, therefore, formed a brilliant spectacle of Shanghai in the field of culture and art.

As for the entertainment in Shanghai, it is quite multifarious and interesting. There are coffee shops, teahouses, bars, karaokes, disco halls, bowling alleys and the golf clubs. China has a long history and brillant culture. For instance, there are many Chinese-style operas (such as the Kunqu opera and the Peking opera) and *quyi* (a folk art form including ballad singing, story-telling, etc.). In such a case, it is quite natural that many attractive programmes are scheduled to have performed by the famous troupes, such as the Shanghai Philharmonic Orchestra, the Shanghai Ballet Troupe, the Shanghai Kunqu Opera Troupe, the Shanghai Peking Opera Troupe, the Shanghai Acrobatic Troupe, the Shanghai Yueju Opera Troupe, the Shanghai Dancing Ensemble and the Old Musicians' Jazz Band at the Peace Hotel. Besides, a great variety of exciting live performance, such as fashion show and popular songs, are often staged in theatres, restaurants, ballrooms and bars.

211.虹口区多伦路文化一条街
Located in Hongkou District, Dulun Road is a well-known cultural street.

212."做一天上海市民"，是一项别出心裁的活动。使来上海的外国游客，有机会直接了解上海市民的日常生活。
"To Be a Shanghainese for One Day". It is one of the interesting programmes prepared for foreign tourists to have a better understanding of the actual life of ordinary Chinese people.

213.Ok,上海!
Ok, Shanghai!

214.亲身感受石库门弄堂里普通老百姓有乐趣的民俗风情
To learn more about the Shanghainese living in the traditional stone-arched-gate residence.

215.初来乍到
The new comers.

# 节庆活动

上海的节庆活动内容丰富，种类繁多，风格独特，气氛热烈，不仅展现了中华民族丰富优秀的文化传统、民俗风情、礼仪风貌，同时也显示了中国人民的聪明才智、美好愿望和审美情趣。

上海常有花会举行，其中最著名的是每年春天的南汇桃花节、上海国际花卉节以及秋天的桂花节。桃花节旨在向游客展示美丽的田园风光，展现纯朴的民情民风，展望新农村美好的发展前景。"亲近大自然，走进桃花源"已成为历届上海桃花节的主题。上海国际花卉节每两年在长风公园举行一次，公园内百万余株奇花异卉给春意盎然的申城增添了无限缤纷的色彩。除了欣赏来自荷兰、日本、美国、新加坡等花卉种植加工大国的国花争奇斗艳外，还有花卉摄影、花谜竞猜、插花比赛、根雕、奇石盆景等一系列以花文化为主题的活动，使国际花卉节内容更为丰富多彩。桂花节以花成名，桂花亦因节而盛，如今，上海桂花节已经成为金秋沪上著名的旅游节庆活动之一。作为活动的主要场所之一的桂林公园，以近二十种桂花名品组成十大花坛，叶重枝密，风来香飘。每到月圆十五夜，中秋赏月赏桂晚会，有景有情，清雅宜人，更有文化展览、文艺演出推波助兴。

龙华庙会，一般自农历三月十五日左右开始，是农历三月上海人游龙华寺，赏桃花的节日盛会。每逢三月，十里桃花，艳若红霞，游人香客纷至沓来。庙会期间，龙华古寺内佛事兴旺，香烟袅袅，佛教音乐悠扬悦耳。龙华古镇上，各种店铺鳞次栉比，买卖兴隆，地方风味小吃特色各异。依寺而建的龙华旅游城，属白墙青瓦的江南民居风格建筑物，洋溢着浓郁的民俗风情。此外，沪剧、越剧、舞龙舞狮、山西绛州锣鼓、安徽花鼓灯、驯兽、河北鸡舞、天

津高跷、沧州大马戏等民俗文艺演出，一定会让您大开眼界。龙华寺的另一项声名远扬的重大节庆活动是每年的岁末除夕，在龙华古寺内举行"迎新年撞龙华晚钟"的活动。每逢除夕，中外游客都会聚集于此，聆听零时的"百八钟声"，在宏亮悠扬的钟声中，迎来吉祥的新年。另有108名幸运游客身披绶带，登上钟楼，与龙华古寺的法师一起撞响"龙华晚钟"。带着佛教意味、诗境意味和神秘意义的钟声，回响在古寺上空，也激荡在人们心中，将最美好的新春祝愿撒向浦江两岸，使中外宾客沉浸在一片欢乐祥和的气氛中。以民族风情为主题的文艺演出、表演，或清雅、或浓烈，与撞钟活动相得益彰。钟楼下殿堂内，香火缭绕，木鱼声起，百余法师祝圣普佛，并出殿"绕佛"，与宾客共祝好运，国富民强，万事如意。

每年正月的豫园元宵灯会则以传统灯展形式，结合现代科技理念，演绎中华传统文化和灯文化，寄予着上海人民企盼国家繁荣、人民安居乐业的美好祝愿。每年农历正月十五的豫园元宵灯会，已成为春节期间沪上老百姓最热闹的去处之一。豫园元宵灯会结合九曲桥的九曲长龙形状和特有水面条件，利用湖心亭与东方明珠遥相呼应的独特优势，体现了上海七百年历史文化新旧对照，寄托着新年的吉祥祝福。将新春的豫园装扮成灯的海洋的数十组大型主题灯组，皆由全国各地著名制作厂商为豫园灯会特别定做，汇集南北各派风格，引入现代科技成果，工艺先进，人物栩栩如生，是颇具民族特色的艺术精品。灯会还将皮影、木偶等艺术形式融入大型灯彩的制作，采用仿古龙灯、脸谱灯、蝴蝶灯、日本宫灯等气氛灯，将艺术性与观赏性融为一体，令人耳目一新。庙戏、斗鸡表演和跳舞机等游戏节目在灯会中集中推出，将令您游兴大增。豫园商城内各特色商店和餐饮店均全面优惠酬宾，使您既能看得赏心、玩得高兴，又能吃得开心、购得放心。豫园商城在九曲桥荷花池，新建了水幕电影表演系统，灯会期间游客可观赏到精彩纷呈、震撼人心的水幕电影表演，她将成为灯会期间一个新的亮点。

上海国际茶文化节是以茶会友，以茶传情，弘扬民族文化的盛大节日。茶文化节的开、闭幕式融

216. 正月初一至初八，举办豫园元宵观灯节。

The programme of watching lanterns in the Yu Garden is held from the 1st day to the 8th of the first lunar month every year.

217. 3 至 4 月举办上海南汇桃花节

The Nanhui Peach Blossom Festival is held in March and April every year.

218. 一年一度的春节

The Spring Festival celebrated every year.

219. 外滩广场陈毅塑像前，经常举办各种别开生面的群众文艺活动。

The statue of Chen Yi (the first mayor of Shanghai) stands on the Bund Square.

表演、敬茶、品茗为一体，体现了茶文化所特有的艺术性和观赏性。闸北公园是茶文化节的主要活动场所，也是人们历来的休闲之处，园内绿树成荫，建有二十处茶文化特色景观，公园门前的"壶王迎客"更是沪上一景。自1994年以来，来自美国、日本、韩国、新加坡、加拿大等十多个国家和香港、澳门地区以及全国各地的茶界人士、茶道代表团、旅游团体和众多市民，参加了历届茶文化节的各项活动。

农历八月十五，是我国传统的中秋节。中秋节亲人团圆是相沿已久的习俗，故俗称"团圆节"。这一天晚上，全家人一边赏月，一边品尝月饼，尽情享受着浓浓的亲情。上海旅游节是集中展示上海都市风光、都市文化、都市商业的大型旅游节庆活动。她以"走进美好与欢乐"为主题，以"人民大众的节日"为定位，在一个月之内集中推出观光、休闲、游园、娱乐、文体、会展、美食、购物等八大类都市旅游特色节目，并以优质服务迎接来自海内外的千百万来宾和游客。

上海旅游节的几项重点项目为国际音乐烟火节、彩车巡游、鲁迅公园"太阳花"英语村、万人单骑游上海、玫瑰婚典、小主人生日游和上海旅游纪念品、消费品博览会等。旅游节期间，您可以欣赏到来自世界各国的烟火艺术家们共同奏响的一曲"火"的交响乐。届时，您将看到璀璨夺目的烟火与流光溢彩、变幻莫测的立体景观交相辉映；您还能在繁华热闹的都市大街以及商业区内看到不同国籍、不同城市、不同风格的彩车组成的流动长龙；您可以在曹杨新村的普通上海人家里和主人聊聊家常，吃上一桌地道的本帮菜肴，体会作一天上海人的感觉；您也可以在闹市中心的人民广场感受上海博物馆厚重的历史文化、上海大剧院现代的高雅艺术、上海城市规划展示馆讲述的上海昨天、今天和明天的故事；您可以在"太阳花"英语村中，寻找到一个良好的交流学习、休憩的园中园；您也可以在衡山路上找到可心的酒吧或茶室，慢慢地品尝着生活的从容；您可以漫步共青森林公园，拥抱绿色，呼吸芬芳，为紧张、疲惫的心灵找寻到一片宁静的

家园；您也可以参加"岩壁上的芭蕾"——攀岩越野挑战赛，挑战自我、战胜自我；您可以参加浪漫激奋的青年聚会——玫瑰婚典，充分体会"活得精彩、爱得精彩、婚礼更精彩"；您也可以让您的孩子参加一个别开生面的"生日聚会"，共同度过一个令人永生难忘的生日；您还可以在上海旅游纪念品、消费品博览会上，看到来自全国各地的旅游纪念品设计生产厂商展示的精美礼品和纪念品……。

除上述几个节庆活动外，上海人还有每年一度的元旦、春节，年轻人的情人节、圣诞节，逢偶数年举办的上海国际艺术节、上海电视节，逢奇数年举办的上海之春音乐会、上海国际电影节以及每年举办的上海国际服装文化节等，所有这些节庆活动，都为上海这座国际性大都市增添了一道亮丽的风景线。

220. 9月至10月，在桂林公园举办上海桂花节。
The Shanghai Sweet-Scented Osmanthus Festival is held at the Guilin Park from September to October every year.

221. 为龙华庙会花灯节制作龙灯
The dragon lanterns are prepared for the Lantern Festival held at the temple fair in Longhua Temple.

222. 舞龙
The dragon dance.

223. 每年的除夕之夜，龙华寺都要举办除旧迎新的撞钟活动，以求万事如意、平安吉祥。
A solemn ceremony of bell-tolling is held every year on the New Year's Eve at the ancient Longhua Temple. The bell is tolled for 108 strokes by an eminent monk, wishing everybody good fortune and long life.

224. 上海民俗文化庙会演出江南丝竹
Traditional stringed and wood wind instruments from the south of the lower reaches of the Yangtze River.

## Various Fesitivals and Programmes in Shanghai

In order to attract more and more tourists from both home and abroad, the Shanghai Tourism Administrations have put foreward over the previous years a series of colourful tours of special interest, including One-day Shanghai Citizen Tour, Museum Tour, Tour of Newly-Weds and Health Protection and Tonic Food Tour. Each of these highly recommended programmes has not only reflected the long history of the Chinese nation, but also demonstrated the wisdom and inspiring desire of the Chinese people.

Flower and plant festivals are held in Shanghai from time to time. Of these festivals, the most popular ones are the Shanghai International Flower and Plant Festival, the Sweet-Scented Osmanthus Festival and the Peach-Blossom Festival held at Nanhui in the Spring every year. With "Close to the Great Nature and Enter into the Peach-Blossom Springs" as its main theme, the Peach-Blossom Festival is initiated from the well-known ideal revealed in a prose narrative written by Tao Yuanming (A.D. 365-427). Held in every other year at the Changfeng Park, the Shanghai International Flower and Plant Festival boasts a wide variety of exotic flowers and rare trees coming from many foreign countries, including the United States, Japan and Singapore. Apart from the appreciation of precious flowers and plants, there are many interesting activities, such as the exhibition of tree-root carvings, the exhibition of queer stones and graceful potted landscapes, and the competition to guess the riddles on the name of certain flowers.

As for the Shanghai Sweet-Scented Osmanthus Festival, it has long been regarded as one of the important tourist activities in Shanghai. Held in the Guilin Park, the festival is noted for having a grand exhibition of many precious varieties of sweet-scented osmanthus flowers. Besides, on the night of the Mid-Autumn Festival(the 15th day of the lunar 8th month), a magnificent evening party is always scheduled to entertain the visitors and guests with a series of interesting performances.

A solemn ceremony of bell-tolling is held every year on the New Year's Eve at the Longhua Tmple. The noted eminent monk Ming Yang joins the tourists in tolling the bell for 108 strokes, wishing everybody good fortune and long life. The most time-honored and grand folk fair in East China is the Longhua Tmple Fair held on the 3rd day of the 3rd month of Chinese lunar calendar. During the fair, Buddhist services are held, Buddhist music is played and the fair is bustled with people. Besides,the local snacks and folk art performances (such as the flower-drum dance from Anhui Province, stilts dance from Tianjin and the chicken dance from Hebei Province) dazzle the audience's eyes.

*Yuanxiao* (the Lantern Festival) falls on the 15th day of the first lunar month. When night has come, people go around in the streets displaying various kinds of fancy lanterns. The well-known Yu Garden Lantern Fair is a real crowd-puller. Embellished with coloured lanterns in the shape of bird, animal and dragon, the place is all the more elegant and intoxicating. Recently, the system of a movie on the water screen is set up nearby the Huxinting Teahouse. Attending the performance of movie, shadow play and puppet is really a high artistic treat.

With the tea as its main media, the Shanghai International Tea Festival is an important occasion to promote the Chinese culture and make friends with all of the foreign visitors. Standing before the entrance to the Zhabei Park, "the King of Teakettles" has usually become a great attraction to the guests coming from other part of the world, including The United States, Japan, South Korea, Canada, Singapore, Macao and Hongkong.

The 15th day of the 8th lunar month is the Mid-Autumn Festival. Those who are away from home always try to get back in time in order to join their kinsmen on that occasion. That's why the festival is known as the family

225

96

225.昆剧——钟馗嫁妹
A scene from the Kunqu opera *Zhong Kui Marries off His Sister.*

226.越剧——红楼梦
A scene from the Yueju opera *A Dream of the Red Mansions.*

227.艺术节一角
A scene from the art festival held in Shanghai.

228.京剧——单刀赴会
*Meeting at the Linjiang Port* (one of the Peking opera repertoires).

229.京剧——穆桂英挂帅
*Mu Guiying Takes Command* (one of the Peking opera repertoires).

97

reunion festival. It is an usual practice for people to get together with all of their family members to admire the full moon while eating moon-cakes.

Recently, there are many new programmes, including the International Music & Fireworks Festival; the float in a parade; the Sunflower English Corner at the Lu Xun Park; the Shanghai Sightseeing by Ten-Thousand Bikes; the Rose Weeding Ceremony; the Happy Birthday Tour and the Shanghai Tourist Souvenir Fair. In this way, if you have come to visit Shanghai on that occasion, you may enjoy a grand display of the best fireworks produced by the famous companies all over the world; you may appreciate the wonderful performance by a gigantic array of floats coming from different countries; you will be invited to become a "honourable resident" of Caoyang Residential Area, having, therefore, an opporturnity to learn the Chinese way of cooking and so on; you will be arranged to visit all of the major museums in Shanghai; you will have a chance to practice English with the local beginners at the English Corner on Sunday morning; you will have the honour to take part in the wedding ceremony of the newly-weds, through which you will eye-witness how the traditional type of wedding ceremonies is carried out in China, and, finally, by way of attending the Shanghai Tourist Souvenir Fair, you will have the chance to find many ideal keepsakes for your kinsmen and friends.

Furthermore, there are also many other interesting activities in Shanghai, such as the New Year's Day, the Spring Festival, the Valentine Day, the Christmas Eve, the Shanghai International Art Festival and the Shanghai TV Festival (held in every even year ), the Concert of Shanghai Spring, the Shanghai International Film Festival (held in every odd year ), and the Shanghai International Fashion Festival. As the showcase of this world-known metropolis, all of these activities will surely make you have a wonderful time.

230

231

**230.豫园龙灯会**
The Dragon and Latern Festival held in the Yu Garden.

**231.罗店龙舟节**
The Dragon Boat Festival held at Luodian.

**232.4月26日至5月2日，在闸北公园举办上海国际茶文化节。**
The Shanghai International Tea Festival is held in Zhabai Park from April 26th to May 2nd every year.

**233.衡山路啤酒屋**
A beer house on Hengshan Road.

**234.玫瑰婚典——庄严、热烈的集体结婚仪式，热恋中的情人在激情中结为夫妻。**
Ceremony of many young couples in Shanghai is often held collectively.

99

# 购物天堂

上海，是中国最繁华的商业中心。拥有100多幢5000平方米以上的大商厦，被誉为"购物天堂"。上海既是国际著名品牌和流行时尚的展示窗口，也云集了大量物美价廉的国产货。这里，既有传统的百年老店、品牌专卖店，也有现代化的百货公司、购物中心，更有超大型的配售中心、仓储式销售店铺；还形成一条从豫园商城到南京路，一直延伸至浦东张杨路的旅游购物专线，让你尽情享受购物的乐趣。

有"中华商业第一街"美誉的南京路，是上海开埠以来建立最早的商业街，它东起黄浦江、西至静安寺与延安西路交叉，横贯上海市中心，全长5.5公里。两侧共有360多家商店，每天约有150万人在街上购物，年销售额20亿元。沿十里长街漫步，商店林立，竞相争辉。入夜，到处霓虹闪烁，橱窗灯火通明。新开通的西起西藏中路东至河南中路的南京路步行街，成为上海的又一城市新景观。

淮海中路，以商品和购物环境的格调高雅著称，素有"穿在淮海路"之称。"巴黎春天"、"百盛购物中心"，已成为黄金地段上含金量最高的商厦。淮海中路上的食品店，多以自产自销正宗的西点为特色。如哈尔滨的面包、老大昌的蛋糕。在雁荡路喝咖啡、在红房子吃"大菜"，是淮海中路特有的优雅情调。

上海人有句熟悉的广告语：看看逛逛其他路，买卖请到四川路。四川北路以中华名品为主，各种日用百货齐全，价位特别适合讲究实惠的工薪阶层。

徐家汇商业城汇集了东方商厦、港汇广场、太平洋百货、第六百货公司、汇金百货等大型集吃、购、玩于一体的百货商厦，高、中、低、廉

商品应有尽有。

被誉为"上海陆上大门一颗明珠"的新客站不夜城，集旅游纪念品、工艺品、土特产和古币、邮票、磁卡于一体。

更有许多游人是冲着"小商品之都"——豫园商城而来。豫园商城以"小、土、特、多"为特色，小到纽扣、瓶塞、手帕、筷子；56家特色商店，商品花色品种多达12000种；还拥有五香豆、梨膏糖、南翔小笼包子等土特产品。

上海的特色商街也很出名，有福州路文化街、华亭路服装街、北京东路五金街、东台路古玩市场、浏河路旧工艺品市场、江阴路花鸟市场等。近年来还出现衡山路酒吧街、雁荡路休闲街、吴江路休闲街、多伦路文化名人街、上海老人街等，为旅游者所青睐。

237

238

235

236

239

235.上海市第一百货股份有限公司
The Shanghai No.1 Department Store.

236.上海中联商厦
The Shanghai Zhonglian Commercial Tower.

237.十里南京路，一个新世界。
A brand-new look of the ten-mile-long Nanjing Road.

238.南京路上的东海商厦
The East Sea Commercial Tower is located on Nanjing Road.

239.先施公司
The Sincere Department Store.

240.南京路步行街
The pedestrian street on Nanjing Road.

241.卖化妆品的导购小姐
A female guide before the cosmetics counter.

242.人民广场地下商城
The Underground Bazzar beneath the People's Square.

## The Paradise for Shoppers

For the Chinese, Shnghai is easily the country's finest shopping centre. For the foreign visitor, too, Shanghai's shops are among the best stocked in the world.

There are more than 500 large-scale department stores in Shanghai. Reputed as a "paradise of shopping", it offers a great variety of consumer goods including the best international brands and the home-made inexpensive commodities. Besides, apart from many established shops, luxury boutiques, modern department stores, upmarkets and the large-scale distribution and retail centres, there is an exclusive shopping route from the Yu Garden Bazzar to Nanjing Road and Zhangyang Road in the Pudong New Area. So, it is sure that the hobby of both the visitors and tourists will be greatly satisfied.

Acclaimed as "the First Street in China", Nanjing Road is the earliest commercial avenue after Shanghai was forced to become an open port in 1843. Divided into two (Nanjing Road East and Nanjing Road West), this busiest of Shanghai's street stretches for nearly ten kilometres (six miles), from the Bund to the Jin'an Temple. Lined with more than 360 grand cinemas, restaurants and shops, it is visited by 1.5 million shoppers every day and the annual income has reached as high as 2,000 millon yuan. In such a case, the street is constantly jammed with pedestrians. And now, with the completion of a grand shopping mall starting from Xizang Road Middle in the west to Henan Road Middle in the east, a brand-new spectacle is thus added to this world-known metropolis.

Noted for luxury goods and favourable environment, Huaihai Road Middle (the Avenue Joffre of old) is reputed as a "place where one can find everything desired in the field of eating, dressing and entertainment". Spread with a series of well-known department stores including the Printemps and the Parkson, it has become one of the prime sec-

243.豫园商城大裕百货
Tianyu Department Store at the Yu Garden Bazzar.

244.豫园商城黄金店
A gold shop at the Yu Garden Bazzar.

245.淮海路美美百货商店
Maison Mode on Huaihai Road Middle.

246~247.豫园商城
Yu Garden Bazzar.

tor in Shanghai. As for the food shops along this avenue, they are renowned for their authentic products. For instance, the bread produced by the Harbin Confectionery and the cake offered by the Laodachang Bakery. Meanwhile, the Cafe Shops on Yandang Road and the Red House Restaurant nearby are the favourite place for those who are keen to the graceful atmosphere and elegant environment.

The flashy Xujiahui shopping district has been established in the vicinity of Xujiahui Cathedral. Furthermore, a massive underground shopping city has been developed under the Renmin Park metro stop, and the stop at the Shanghai Railway Station is adjacent to one of the brightest, most modern malls in Shanghai.

Shanghai is an ideal "paradise for shoppers". Shanghai's commerce has been wellknown for its long history, large number of shops, variety of goods and quality service. Its handicrafts, souvenirs and small articles for daily use are getting more and more popular among Chinese and foreign visitors for their national characteristics, local style and excellent workmanship. The Nanjing Road, Huaihai Road, Jinling Road, Sichuan Road North, Xizang Road and YuGarden Bazaar are all dotted with shops which have abundant commodities for sale and a multitude of shoppers. These streets can be called the busiest business sections in China. Overseas visitors say that Shanghai has available a collection of all famous, special, new and high-quality products and has combined the functinos of sightseeing with shopping and eating. All shopping needs can be met here. Shanghai is indeed a paradise for shoppers, Chinese or foreign, at all levels to their satisfaction.

248.淮海路商业中心远眺
A distant view of the commercial center on Huaihai Road.

249.淮海路之夜
The Night at Huaihai Road.

250.友谊商店
The Friendship Store.

251.浦东第一八佰伴新世纪商厦中式商业厅
The Business Hall in Traditional Chinese Style at the New Century Tower in the Pudong New Area.

252.全国土产食品商店
The National Local Product Shop.

253.淮海路上的益民食品店
Yiming Food Shop on Huaihai Road .

254

255

256

259

260

261

264

265

254~260.多彩的橱窗
The colorful show windows.

261.汉光陶艺馆
Hanguang Ceramics Museum

262.每年一度的华东地区出口商品交易会
The Shanghai East China Export Commodity Fair is held every year.

263.外国游客选购艺术挂毯
The foreign visitors are selecting the art tapestry.

264.上海东方商厦有限公司
Shanghai Oriental Commercial Company Ltd.

265~266.徐家汇商业中心年销售额超过南京路
The total selling of Xujiahui Commerial Centre surpasses that of Naijing Road.

267

268

269

267.美国前总统克林顿1998年到上海证券交易所

In 1998, Mr Klinton, the former US president, visited the Shanghai Stock Exchange.

268.中国外汇调剂中心

The China Foreign Exchange Redistribution Centre.

269.上海证券交易所

The Shanghai Stock Exchange.

270.上海金属交易所，年交易量占世界第三位。

The Shanghai Metal Exchange Centre.

271.宝大祥公司

Baodaxiang Silk Company.

272.朵云轩画廊和古玩店

Duoyunxuan Picture and Antique Store.

273.创建于康熙元年的雷允上国药号

Lei Yun Shang Chinese Medicine Store was established in the first year of the reign of Emperor Kangxi during the Qing Dynasty.

274.建于1783年的童涵春堂国药号

Tonghanchun Chinese Medicine Store was established in 1783.

# 美食乐园

上海，因其优越的地理位置，为地方风味菜提供了极为丰富、优良的烹饪加工原料。1843年，上海开埠，各地帮菜很快齐集上海，为上海地方菜的发展，提供了技术、品种等诸多方面的借鉴。上海地方菜，在坚持以本地居民口味为主的前提下，兼收并蓄，吸取各帮的长处，不断丰富和充实自身的品种和烹调方法。

上海地方风味菜，以烹制河鲜、海鲜、禽、畜和时令菜蔬著称，烹调方法有红烧、炸、炒、爆、生煎、生煸、蒸、糟、煨、油焖等，主要味别有咸鲜、咸甜、甜酸、咸辣、甜辣、糟香，菜肴朴实素雅，注重原味，甜咸适宜，浓淡兼长，清醇和美。著名菜肴有糟鸡、白切肉、油爆虾、扇形甩水、红烧河鳗、红烧鲑鱼、青鱼秃肺、鸡骨酱、八宝辣酱、八宝鸭、虾子大乌参、扣三丝、生煸草头、肉丝黄豆汤等，都具有浓郁的乡土气息，颇受本地居民的喜爱。

现在供应的许多著名上海地方风味菜肴中，有的是有数百年历史的地方传统菜，如名菜"糟钵头"，在二百多年前已是上海地方名菜。当然，现在供应的"糟钵头"和二百年前的"糟钵头"相比，无论在投料和用器上，都有较大的改变。如现在的"糟钵头"配料用油豆腐、冬笋片，有的还加细粉；原来用钵头，现在用砂锅等。但其浓醇、鲜肥、芳香的特色，依然如故，所以，至今仍为广大消费者所称颂。

在上海地方风味菜中，用香糟的品种也有不少，如冷菜中的糟鸡、糟肉、糟肚、糟猪脚、糟凤爪、糟豆荚、糟冬笋等等。热菜中也有很多用糟的品种，而用糟的方法也较多样。近年在传统糟类品种基础上，开发的"糟氽蝴蝶鱼"和"香糟鱼尾"，因原料经无盐糟腌，成品汤汁清澈，肉质鲜嫩，糟味更加芳香。

110

275.上海老饭店新址，位于豫园福佑路，外观和整个豫园商城的仿明清建筑风格相一致。上海地方风味菜注重原味，甜咸适宜，浓淡兼长，清醇和美。

The Shanghai-Cuisine Restaurant in the Yu Garden is renowned all over China.

276.南翔小笼包子

The Nanxiang stuffed buns cooked in bamboo steamers.

277.豫园商城正宗奶油五香豆专卖店

The shop selling creamy spiced beans at the Yu Garden Bazzar.

278."菜篮子"工程的产业化、市场化水平进一步提高。

The Shopping Basket Programme, a result of the municipal government's great concern for the people.

279.豫园小笼包子店

Nanxiang stuffed buns in the Yu Garden are renowned all over China for their ingenuity.

280.生煎馒头

The stuffd buns being fried in shallow oil.

281.蟹黄烧麦

The reddish-yellow crab meat *shaomai* (a steamed dumpling with the dough gathered at the top).

282.香菇菜包

The steamed stuffed buns with mushrooms and vegetables.

283.萝卜丝酥饼

Flaky crackers with radish slices as their stuffing.

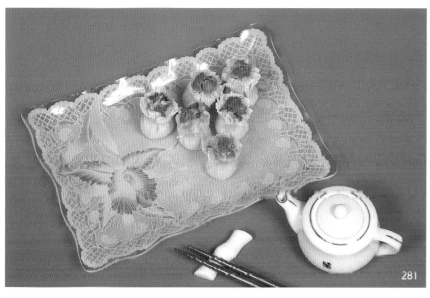

284.红油明虾
Braised shrimps.

285.菊香蟹肥
Crab meat steamed with chrysanthemum.

上海现约有2000多家小吃店铺和摊头，供应的品种繁多，琳琅满目，造型精致，味美可口，仅每天早餐的点心就有300多种。上海的小吃点心，除本地方风味点心外，还有来自江、浙、京、广等地方风味特色点心和具有英、法、德、意、俄特点的西式点心。上海著名的风味小吃有：南翔小笼馒头，即小笼肉包，以豫园商城内的南翔馒头店和西藏路延安路口的古猗园点心店最为有名。其特点是小巧玲珑，晶莹透明，上口一包汤汁，满口生津，回味无穷。鸽蛋圆子，以豫园桂花厅点心店经营的最有特色，圆子洁白形似鸽蛋，煮熟后糯软滑润，入口香甜清凉，是夏令应时佳点。排骨年糕，产于四川中路小常州点心店和西藏南路鲜得来点心店，排骨香酥鲜嫩，年糕香糯适口。此外还有擂沙圆子、生煎馒头、葱油面、眉毛酥、小绍兴鸡粥、桂花糯米糖粥、鲜肉猫耳朵、鸡鸭血汤、枣泥酥、面筋百叶等。

目前，上海已汇集京、粤、苏、扬、锡、甬(宁波)、杭、闽、川、徽、潮、湘、鲁、豫、东北等地方菜，加上素食菜、清真菜，还有英、法、意、德、日、俄、美、墨西哥、巴西、印度、新加坡、泰国、韩国、越南等国的菜肴、点心以及上海本帮菜共30余个帮别。另外，还有肯德基、麦当劳、必胜客、汉堡包等众多西式快餐，时兴的有中式新亚快餐。上海遂成为包罗万象的美食乐园，吃在上海，享受在上海，已是中外嘉宾最美好的心愿。

284

285

286.清炒鳝糊
Stir-fried eel paste.

287.八宝鸭
Eight treasure (choice ingredients of certain special dishes) duck.

288.火夹桂鱼
Baked salmon.

289.上海玉佛寺的素斋
The vegetable dish in the Jade Buddha Temple.

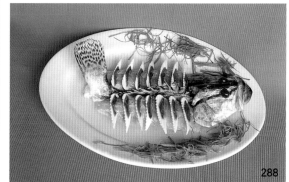

The culinary art in China has a long history. There are many distinguished regional cuisines throughout the country, including Guangdong, Sichuan, Fujian, Shandong, Zhejiang, Jiangsu and Anhui. Ever since the establishment of Shanghai as an open trade port in 1843, a good number of noted chefs of various regional cuisine moved to Shanghai from their native places. As a result, on the basis of absorbing the strong points of the famous regional cuisines of Hangzhou, Suzhou, Ningbo and Yangzhou, the unique feature of Shanghai cuisine is gradually formed. Besides, in order to ensure the quality and flavour peculiar to their own traditional cuisine, the Shanghai chefs have invented a series of new cooking skills, such as to braise in soy sauce; to stir-fry; to steam; to quick-fry or to cook over a slow fire. And now, noted for a great variety of delicious dishes made of the live acquatic product and fresh vegetables, the Shanghai cuisine boasts the following well-received dishes: the braised shrimps; the eight treasures (choice ingredients of certain special condiments) duck; the white cut pork and the chicken with distillers' grains.

Among a lot of authentic Shanghai dishes, the representative one is none other than the dish produced with *jiuzao* (distillers' grains). For instance, as early as more than two hundred years ago, the *zaobendou* (the hotpot with distillers' grains) had long become one of the famous dishes in Shanghai. As one of the cold dishes in the menu of Shanghai cuisine, it include the following well-received titles: the slices of winter bamboo shoots with distillers' grains, the chicken with distillers' grains and the cut pork with distillers' grains.

However, though all of the choice ingredients (such as the slices of winter bamboo shoots and

290

291

114

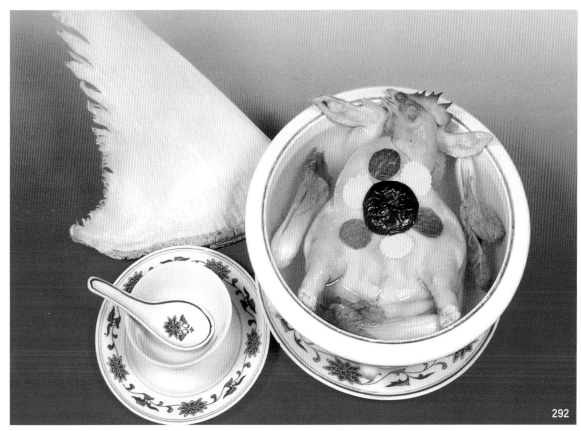

290.糟毛豆
Fresh soya beans with distillers' grains.

291.青鱼秃肺
Black carp steamed

292.鸡包排翅
Spareribs and chicken wings.

293.腌汆暖锅
The quick boil hotpot with different meat and pickles.

294.走油扣肉
Braised large cuts of meat.

295.葱油萝卜丝
The radish slices fried with onions.

紫金山大酒店汇海餐厅，汇集千般美味，海纳万种风情，将法式大餐、日本料理、韩国烧烤、东南亚美点、意大利比萨、印度薄饼等正宗美食溶于一体。

A bar at Huihai Restaurant under Zijinshan Hotel. This restaurant is noted for offering a great variety of foreign cuisines, including French, Japanese, South Korean, Italian and Indian.

296.脆皮烤三纹鱼
Roast sanwen fish.

297.香草薄荷汁烤羊架
Roast mutton with vanilla peppermint.

298.波士顿龙虾色拉
Boston lobsters and salad.

299.烙丁香火腿
Baked ham in lilac flavour.

the vermicelli made from bean starch) remain all the same, the container of this wellknown dish has been changed from *bendou* (earthen bowl) to *shagou* (earthware pot).

Shanghai snacks are renowned all over China for their ingenuity and variety. At present, there are more than two thousand snack shops and stalls, offering a countless array of inexpensive local snacks, such as soya-bean milk, deep-fried twisted dough sticks and large flatbreads. The most famous snack in Shanghai is the Nanxiang stuffed bun produced by the long-established shop at the Yu Garden Bazzar. As for the spare-ribs and *niangao* (New Year cake made of glutinous rice flour), the best brand is produced the Little Changzhou Snack Shop on Sichuan Road Middle and by the Xiandelai (Delicious) Snack Shop on Xizang Road South. Of course, there are also a lot of local snacks (such as the duck blood soup and the dumplings made of glutinous rice flour served in soup) highly recommended by the gourmets from both home and abroad.

Recently, in addition to the successive appearance of a series of forign pastry shops and Western-style restaurants, there emerge one after the other many world-known fast food shops, including the Pizza Hut, the Kentuky Fried Chicken outlet and the McDonald's. In this way, Shanghai has become now the "Gourmets' Paradise"in reality as well as in name. So, a good number of tourists put it that "One can really enjoy all the dishes under heaven in Shanghai."

# 宾馆饭店 Major Hotels

300.华亭宾馆
Hua Ting Guest House.

301.上海宾馆咖啡厅
A coffe house in the Shanghai Hotel.

302.锦沧文华大酒店
Shanghai JC Mandarin.

303.银河宾馆
Galaxy Hotel.

304.金沙江大酒店
Jinsha Hotel.

305.白玉兰宾馆大厅
The lobby of Magnolia Guest House.

306.上海万豪虹桥大酒店大堂
The lobby of Shanghai Wanhao Hongqiao Hotel.

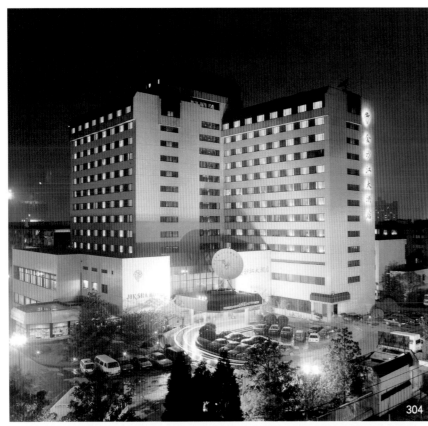

307.上海万豪虹桥大酒店游泳池
A swimming pool in the Shanghai Wanhao Hongqiao Hotel.

308.和平饭店贵宾厅
A honorable guest hall in Peace Hotel.

309.扬子江大酒店
Yangtze New World.

310.紫金山大酒店是四星级酒店，位于浦东新区东方路，距浦东国际机场约30分钟车程，是一座具有国际一流水准的商务、旅游酒店。

Located on Dongfang Road in Pudong New Area, Zijinshan Hotel is a four-star hotel. It is only 30-minute-drive away from the Pudong International Airport.

311.新锦江大酒店
Jinjiang Tower.

312.太平洋大酒店
Pacific Hotel.

313.城市酒店
City Hotel.

# 上海市旅游示意图
## Tourist Sketch Map of Shanghai